The Real Estate Professional's Handbook for Starting and Running a Successful Business

The Real Estate Professional's Handbook for Starting and Running a Successful Business

Tim A. Baker

PUBLISHING

New York

Editorial Director: Jennifer Farthing
Development Editor: Joshua Martino
Production Editor: Julio Espin
Typesetting: the dotted i
Cover Design: Rod Hernandez

Published by Kaplan Publishing
A Division of Kaplan Inc.

June 2007
07 08 09 10 9 8 7 6 5 4 3 2 1

ISBN 13: 978-1-4277-5466-0
ISBN 10: 1-4277-5466-7

Contents

Acknowledgements

There have been many individuals who have affected my understanding of my real estate career. One of the first who had an influence on me was Bob Schiller of Schiller Real Estate in Elmhurst, Illinois. He remains a good friend. It was there that I received my first instructions. Schiller Real Estate is still a major player in the real estate business in that area. Many of my friends whom I met there gave me their advice and assistance as I embarked on this new venture. Bob has served in many capacities for the Association of Realtors and is a major mentor for many agents today.

The next place I went to was Naperville, Illinois, and worked with a Coldwell Banker office under the tutelage of Char Parker. She also remains a friend to this day though she owns a company under a different franchise now. She took a chance on this upstart in the business who was at the time still teaching full time.

Eventually I joined the RE/MAX office in Naperville with Jack Brennan as the broker. Ultimately I tried my hand at owning a RE/MAX office with two associates, Rosemary Wisnosky and Nancy Schaaf.

After 20 years of being in the business in Illinois we went back to an area that we had lived in for a short time, Arizona. We decided to move to Tucson though we owned a condo in Scottsdale. Our oldest daughter would be having our first grandchild there. Eventually all of our children moved to Arizona.

I stayed with the RE/MAX brand and hired a partner, Graham Glauser. We purchased an agent's business with great success and have enjoyed the opportunity to grow in the Tucson market. We recently purchased a team in Casa Grande, Arizona, from some good friends and will be continuing to enhance their already well-established business. Our plan is to establish a third team in a growth area about halfway between our office in Tucson and our office in Casa Grande.

There is great excitement in developing and growing a real estate business. It takes time and effort but it remains the most lucrative and fulfilling venture I could have dreamed of being involved with.

With the help of several mentors along the way I have received the coaching and the direction that I have needed. The most memorable of these coaches are Dr Fred Grosse and Howard Brinton. It has been a wonderful adventure and one in which I feel I have gained knowledge that is able to be shared with those who are just embarking on this journey.

At some point there will be a change in my plans and I will be the one looking to exit from the real estate marathon in which I have been entrenched. When that time comes I want to be able to benefit from the hours, days, and years I have invested. In the meantime I will enjoy all of the privileges that this business affords me. The travel to distant lands, the association with the highest level of professionals in our industry, and the deep friendships that this affiliation has engendered are but a few of the benefits that have been mine over the years.

Introduction

I wish that I had known then what I know now. In 1979, I entered the real estate business thinking that it was a job, not a business. I made no plans. I created no budget. My only goal was to make some extra money to supplement my teaching income. I was sure that with a little effort on weekends, evenings, and summer holidays, I could earn sufficient dollars to satisfy my needs. I was typical of most new agents coming into the field of real estate sales. I had no vision of what it would take to create a successful real estate practice.

I found myself stumbling through the process, reacting to stimuli around me instead of creating the type of environment in which I was in charge of my future. Someone would come up with a new marketing ploy, and I would sign on the dotted line, giving away pre-earned dollars to this vision someone else had for the development of new clients. Some things worked. Some things didn't work. I had no accurate way to gauge the difference.

My plan for future income was on a month-by-month basis. If I had an upcoming expense, I worked a bit harder to find a buyer or seller to work with. When my needs were not so great, my efforts seemed to dwindle accordingly. My first broker said that he loved to see his agents have a big purchase in their near future. Now I know why.

The income stream seemed to have many peaks and valleys. There were times of drought and times of plenty. I was unable to make things happen in a consistent way. Although there may be seasons in which the market flows more generously, I have found that the taller peaks and deeper valleys were my own creation.

Over the years, I had mentors who taught me the basic principles to develop a successful real estate business. I found that some of their procedures for success were tedious, at first. It took time to develop the discipline to follow these simple systematic tasks that invariably create constancy to the enterprise.

Now, income streams are predictable. The cost of doing business is easy to monitor. The stress and strain of being a commission-based income provider became a new-found freedom of choices because of the unequaled abundance this vocation provides, both in dollars and in time.

In this book, I am sharing with you what took me years to learn. You will not need so much time. You will not make my mistakes. You will be able to create, in significantly shorter time than it took me, an opportunity that will provide you satisfaction, wealth, and time for personal growth. You will be able to place the most important people and experiences on your life calendar where they belong: first. Your career in real estate will provide the necessary funding to put them there.

Please don't misinterpret these statements. This book and its contents are not a magic pill. They are simply an outline for disciplined, systematic procedures which will guide your vision, initiative, entrepreneurship, and management skills towards the fulfillment of the dream. It will still take effort. There will still be the requisite learning opportunities. You'll still need to invest your time.

What you will build is a business that has value. Far too many fine agents have walked away when they no longer feel that real estate is for them. They have left by the wayside a valuable asset, cast aside as if it has no worth.

Another will pick up where you decide to leave off. You can take a step back in responsibility and be a part of the new future or you may provide the new business owner with all the power to make it what he or she decides it can become. In the meantime, you will take with you the income that will fund the next vision you decide to create.

The tools are here for you to utilize. You may decide it is more effort than you want to expend. If that is your choice, then you may find yourself as part of the 80 percent of practitioners in the field of real estate who seem to have no destination in sight. When they decide to leave the enterprise there is nothing of lasting value left behind.

It is your choice. Choose well.

1

What Are You Doing Here, Anyway?

Why are you going into the field of real estate? What makes this field your chosen field? Who talked you into it? What about the opportunity excites you? Is it your first choice in a career? Did something else not work to your satisfaction, so you thought you would give real estate a chance? Are you part-time or full-time?

Everyone has their own reasons for making this career move. For some, it is a solid choice based on a systematic investigation of the advantages and disadvantages. They examine their strengths that will help them succeed. As a result, they enter the field with confidence and determination.

Unfortunately, many are like me. I was a teacher. I needed supplemental income to support my teaching career. I was sure that I could make some decent income working weekends, holidays, and summers. It appeared to be a not-too-difficult way to give me some added income. Besides, real estate is the American Dream. Everyone wants to own a home.

How hard could it be, anyway? You sit in an office. The phone rings. Some nice person wants to buy or sell a home.

You meet with them, fill out some paperwork, and go to a closing. What could be easier?

Certainly, the brokers would all be willing to give you the training and support that you need. Everyone in the office would want to help you become successful. They would each be willing to share their secrets of success. The broker would eagerly supply all of the advertising, Web sites, phones, stamps, stationery, envelopes, forms, office supplies, and space in which to conduct your business. A full cadre of staff would stuff envelopes, follow through on your files, and handle any overload that might occur.

Then reality hits: it's your responsibility to make things happen. But once that bit of truth sinks in, you may find that the field you have chosen is fun, challenging, and potentially lucrative.

When you decide to enter real estate, you are entering a world of opportunity. There are no limits on the size of your dream. No one will slow you down unless you let them. A proactive approach to planning your future will create limitless avenues for success and the fulfillment of your personal vision for life.

Why Real Estate?

Real estate sales is a field requiring many assets on the part of the agent. Certainly the first requirement is that you want to be around people and work with them. This part of the business would seem to be fairly well understood. However, the sarcastic phrase, "This would be a great career if it weren't for the people," crops up fairly often.

People are the center of the business. Land and homes are simply a commodity that we put on the shelves of the real estate store. Your task is to assist people in the procurement and sale of some form of real estate. Their desires are the focal point of the business. It does not matter what you might want them to purchase or sell. Their wants and needs, their definitions of what is significant, and their capacity to buy or their impetus to sell will dictate the requirements of the transaction.

With some individuals, you'll just click. Their professed way of life is in sync with yours, and their needs are easily filled. Then with others, you will need to adjust your approach to work with them effectively. You need to understand the variety of personalities and the styles of communication that make each person feel comfortable with the relationship and with the transaction. The task of the real estate agent is to meet the needs of the client, not have the client meet the agent's needs.

Another requirement is a good work ethic. This is not a business for those looking for the easy life. You must put in long hours to get started in this business. Certainly the longer you are in the business, the less time maintaining a certain level of production will take. The question remains, "What level of production do I feel comfortable maintaining?" Until you reach that level, you will invest time, effort, and money to increase productivity.

Real estate sales provides a wonderful opportunity to create a business that can fund your life. This opportunity depends primarily on setting goals to meet your desired level of success. You do not have to meet the goals of an employer. Instead, this is your business, for which you are the key stockholder. The dividends depend on how effectively you plan your business and how well you implement the plan.

Yet another essential ingredient is persistence. Some agents have trouble believing that not everyone wants to employ their services. Some potential clients have friends or relatives in the business with whom they'd rather work. Others only want to work with the number-one agent in the business. Because there can only be one of those, you either are or aren't that individual. If you are not that person, then you will need persistence to join that upper tier of agents who have found a category in which they're number one.

Persistence means continuing to do those things that will bring you success, even though success does not occur instantaneously. It takes consistency to develop into the agent of choice for a large enough group of people to sustain your desired level of business. Persistence means that you will work through disappointments until you achieve your planned level of success.

My son entered the real estate business two years ago. When he started, he came to me to find out what he should do to achieve the success he desired. We sat down and developed a plan and a budget for the plan. Part of the plan included his selection of a "farm" area in which to cultivate long-term business relationships. He selected several subdivisions in the Queen Creek, Arizona, area and began the process of delivering notepads with a letter attached. He expected that the phone calls would come immediately. They did not. He called me to find out why the effort didn't seem to be paying off. I informed him that he was in for a long-term commitment. If he continued to do the things we had built into the plan, then the results would turn out the way we had expected. I needed him to be patient and persistent.

I reminded him of a story from when he was a child. We would go for walks. If I got too far ahead, he would stop. He would wait for me to come back to him, and then we would move on. One day, I kept going and turned the corner. I was out of sight and certain that he would be along any second. After about two minutes, I went back and peeked around the corner. He was standing in the exact spot where he had stopped two minutes earlier. I finally went back to him so we could continue the walk. His position was persistent in spite of the circumstances.

He decided to continue delivering the notepads. People called, thanked him for the notepads, and asked if he could list their homes. Because he was persistent, his plans met with continued success. He had over 35 transactions during his first full year in the business.

Persistence means continuing to do the things that other real estate agents do not want to do. My son went door to door delivering notepads. It took time and effort. Some days were hot, up to 110 degrees. In spite of the heat and the time he had to spend, he found success through his persistence.

The 80/20 Rule

I work in the Tucson, Arizona, market. In 2005, there were 6,536 members of the Tucson Association of Realtors Multiple Listing Service. Statistics show that 2,631 members produced no closed transactions that year. It is true that some appraisers are members of the MLS. It is also true that members of teams do not show transactions under their own MLS identification number; about 350 of them would fall into that classification. That still leaves 2,281 agents who had no transactions for the entire year.

In addition, 522 agents had closed just one transaction for the year; another 501 had closed only two transactions; and only 387 had closed three transactions.

If you assume that 350 of these agents are team members or appraisers, then 3,691 agents, or 56.5 percent of the MLS members, closed three or fewer transactions for 2005. A full 80 percent of the members had one closed transaction a month or less. By the time you get to two closed transactions per month, you are down to 4 percent of the membership.

This kind of production is typical across the country. According to reports from the National Association of Realtors, the average number of sales is eight per agent. These statistics should give new agents a reason to pause and ponder their future.

What does it take to reach the top 20 percent? How many transactions do you need to close to earn an adequate return for your investment of time and money? What will it take to fulfill your dream?

The 80/20 rule says that 20 percent of the sales force will do 80 percent of the business. The last 20 percent of the business is divided by 80 percent of the agents. Obviously, many licensed real estate agents do not earn a substantial amount of money. The fact that 80 percent of agents have left the business within their first two years of becoming licensed poses an important question for the new agent: How much determination do you have to complete the task and become a part of the upper tier of agents?

Nobody goes into real estate to be mediocre. This book will give you the ability to be a top agent should you choose to adopt its philosophy, systems, and methodology.

In 2005, in a seller's market, our team closed 309 transactions. Then in 2006, in a more even market for buyers and sellers, our team still set its sight on closing over 250 transactions.

A Job or a Business?

Earlier, I mentioned that I entered the field of real estate sales as if it were a regular job with a boss who would demand that I meet certain goals. Real estate introduced me to the term *independent contractor.* I had no idea what it meant and how it might be different from the word *employee.*

I had always been an employee. I had never been given the freedom and responsibility to create my own business. I did not understand that if "it's going to be, it's up to me." I thought if it was going to be, the boss would tell me how to accomplish it.

Not many agents entering the field of real estate realize that they will be entrepreneurs who must create a business of their own. They rarely comprehend that they will own it, run it, pay for it, and—ideally—have it as an asset at the end of a long and successful experience.

With proper training, the new or long-term agent can establish a well-planned, well-engineered, self-perpetuating business that will bring opportunities for personal and financial growth unparalleled in other business settings. The horizon is limitless. The walls of the "job" just need to be toppled so that the immense space of "business" can be visualized.

Your perspective will change when you realize that you own your own business. Plans will emerge. New spurts of energy will arise. You will no longer feel trapped by the boss' vision. You will need to work with a broker who relishes your zest for the real estate business that is now yours. You will need to develop a business plan and systematically develop the methods to run your business like clockwork.

CHAPTER

2

Who Are You?

Before you start developing your business plan, you must identify who you are and what part you play best in this business. That may seem like a philosophical question unrelated to your new venture, but it is actually at the center of any planning. Unless you understand who you are and what part you are most comfortable playing, your journey will be marred by haphazard forays into the unknown, untried, and uncomfortable.

D Personality

Are you very competitive? Do you like to always be number one? Are you direct? Do you find lengthy explanations frustrating? Is your undercurrent of thought "Give me the facts, and do it quickly—I need to make a decision"? If disagreements occur, do you find yourself forgetting about them nearly as soon as they are over? If you answered yes to these questions, you could be a D personality.

Ds tend to move quickly through any process, making informed but quick decisions. They are not interested in lengthy catalogs of information presented in what feels like a lot of time. They want to get to the point, make the decision, and move on to the next topic. Ds tend to be entrepreneurs with a visionary drive, an underlying competitiveness, and a strong sense of destiny.

I Personality

Perhaps instead you find yourself with that sense of competition but also a desire to develop and maintain relationships. You may find that you need deeper levels of communication with those around you. Relationship building may be an art form for you. Also, living in the nicer neighborhood, driving the car that conveys status, or having your children attend better schools may be priorities.

If these attributes seem to fit, you may well have a strong I personality. Is love to have relationship-based business endeavors. If you are an I, being around people and knowing that they respect you is a big part of your daily perception of well-being. Is find comfort in social settings. It is difficult for Is to accept rejection; they view fallen relationships as failures.

C Personality

Do you like detail? Do you line up the pencils on your desk by size? Is precision your goal? Does inadequate information on a topic feel like a drought? Do you actually thirst for more input? Do you feel that inadequate information gives you a picture too incomplete to make a well-thought-out decision? If so, then you show signs of having a C personality.

Precise, detailed information is the lifeblood of a C. Engineers, statisticians, and mathematicians are often Cs. A businessperson with a C personality is prone to gather a great deal of information before making any decision. The decision will end up very calculated, well planned, and thoroughly informed. Cs have a hard time enjoying the same agenda as a D.

S Personality

Do you enjoy playing the backup role? Do you revel in providing support? Are you family oriented with pictures of your loved ones adorning your desk? Do you see yourself as the anchor of the team, making sure that everything is snugly packaged for precision team response? At the end of the day, does your desk look as though no one sat there? Is it important to have a place for everything and have everything in its place? You may be an S.

Ss are stabilizers. Their world requires consistency. Change is not the best ally for an S. When the task is understood, an S will find a way to accomplish the task with the least amount of disruption. They love to provide systematic methods of organizing their worlds. The public is soothed by the emotional stability of the S, and the S is soothed by knowing they have done a good job, meeting or exceeding expectations.

The Personality Inventory Test

These personality types and their descriptions are based on the DiSC® personality inventory profiles. This is not a pass/fail test. This is a tool to help you understand yourself and understand how others, who may have different personality profiles from yours, function. No personality profile is a negative. Each personality brings strength to the business relationship. (DiSC is a registered trademark of Inscape Publishing, Inc. Materials can be ordered via the Internet through Inscape or its licensed vendors.)

You may have a strong feeling about which personality style you demonstrate most dominantly. It is, however, advisable to make arrangements to take the test and receive a written profile. It will help you to understand the feelings you have expressed through your answers on the test.

This process will increase your understanding of who you are. Remember that knowing who you are and how you function at peak proficiency with the most comfort is the goal. When you reach this goal, the tasks that you can perform to maximize your value become apparent. You will undoubtedly find that you feel most competent at these tasks.

I am a flaming I. As with most Is, I am not proficient at dealing with paperwork. My desk at the end of the day appears to have been undone by a hurricane. Others shudder. I simply hire Ss and Cs to take care of the critical paper work. They know where it is when I need it. When they go home at night, I can sit at their clean desks and feel enormously comfortable. At their desks, I have space for my papers and a flat space to write on. It is wonderful. I am getting better. Lately, my office only looks as though a gentle tornado has been through it.

I could spend the rest of my life bemoaning my inadequacies, but that would be a waste of time. Instead, I hire individuals who are equipped with the traits that I lack. Then I get to do what I do best. I am the rainmaker. I make sure that calls are coming in to the team. I use my years of experience in selling to train those with less experience. They have the sails. I am the wind.

Loner or CEO

Many individuals prefer to be in charge of every aspect of the business, working hands-on. Others prefer to organize a group to deal with tasks. It is important to figure out how you like to operate.

Part of your business planning will involve deciding how much you want to do and how much you can do efficiently by yourself. This does not mean that you must hire an immense staff and become the super-manager. It does mean that you can choose to work on your own but not by yourself.

With limited time each day, you need an assortment of people who can assist you. You may use the staff provided by your broker to handle some mailings or employ the office transaction coordination staff to take care of the more mundane tasks. You may decide to have an assistant on whom you can rely to handle matters in the way you direct.

Personally handling every call and every piece of paper will be, at best, time consuming, and it will put you in the position of doing less productive projects when your real responsibility is to be meeting with buyers and sellers. Working independently does not mean that you work alone. It simply means that you have a greater degree of control, because you involve fewer individuals in the process.

As a single agent, you will find that time becomes a critical issue. You will spend proportionately more time the more you grow your business. Each contract or listing requires a certain time commitment. The more contracts and listings you have in hand, the more time will be required to complete them. Because each of us is given only 24 hours in a day, you will need to organize yourself so that you hum along at a fine-tuned pace.

Even the most talented organizers find that they may need an additional arm or leg. If you are one of these individuals, locate an assistant in whom you have the ultimate confidence to carry out your directives as efficiently as you would handle them. If you are an independent type, it will not be easy for you to yield tasks to someone else. Thus, your operation will be nearly hands-on but with the assistance of a very trusted associate. When such teams are in motion, they demonstrate precision at its best.

The other approach is to find individuals who are able and excited to do what you find unpleasant or impossible to complete given your skill sets and personality. You become what we refer to as the "rainmaker." You have the vision for where the team can go but realize your own limitations in getting there as a solo agent.

With the rainmaking approach, you will have to let go a little bit and realize that ideas, concepts, and insights that come from the team can streamline the process of caring for the clients. This approach involves delegating authority to make decisions to others. It requires management skills that must be honed and developed over time. It is often a matter of being able to work more *on* the business than *in* the business. The members of the team do the hands-on work. As the CEO, you are the general overseer, while the members of your team are responsible for the more specific tasks.

I find great fulfillment in providing an opportunity for members of my team to grow and advance. Our goal for licensed field agents is to have each of them at a six-figure income annually. The administrative staff is committed to the success of the team. They design and develop new systems to enhance communication with and provide better service to our clients.

The Real Estate Cycle

The real estate cycle is the map for designing the systems to handle each aspect of the business. The cycle is divided into three main parts. Part one is the creation of the business. Part two is the execution of the business. Part three is the processing of the business.

Part One

Part one is the most difficult for agents. The question is, "How do I get the attention of people who need to buy or sell real estate?" There are many ways to create the awareness in the general public that you

- are a licensed real estate agent;
- are well prepared to handle their needs;
- understand the market in which they have an interest;
- are prepared to spend the time necessary to handle their needs; and
- are easily accessible.

General messages sent to the public all at once can create a fire hose effect. The leads can come in at a pace that is unreasonable for you to handle. If the public's perception is that you are too busy to get back to them, handle their needs, and follow up, then all your efforts yield negative results. On the other hand, if you do nothing to get your name and information into the hands of others, then even your closest friends won't know that you are in the business. You need to plan a steady release of your information to the public so that the flow is neither a drought nor a flood.

Part Two

Once the calls come in from potential clients, you must structure your time so that you can meet with them and view their home if they want to sell, or take them out to see the available inventory that meets their criteria if they want to buy. Preparation for one-on-one experience with the client is more sophisticated than ever. To confirm loyalty throughout the transaction, you must provide them with a sense of confidence in your capabilities professionally and your desire to service their needs. Meeting with people but not meeting their needs or not instilling confidence is a waste of their time and yours. What is your success rate in transforming a potential client into a past client? How many chances are you getting to perform face-to-face? When you have that opportunity, how efficient are you at handling a client's need?

Some agents end up with many appointments but few clients. If you have too many appointments to handle, you won't do well with any of them. Some agents have too few appointments, and they communicate a need to gain business rather than a need to serve the client. When you focus on the clients' needs while you are with them, they will gain confidence in your abilities and professionalism and the relationship will prosper.

Part Three

Once the client has successfully found the right home or the right buyer, much still needs to be done. The agent has the responsibility of assisting the client with meeting contractual time lines and responsibilities. In some states, you organize these responsibilities with an attorney. In other states, you spend time directing the work with the lender, title company, home inspector, pest inspector, home owners' association, septic inspectors, radon inspectors, repair personnel, and many other individuals who are involved in the consummation of the contract. In addition, you will likely deal with another agent who is involved with the same individuals.

The jobs may appear endless, and it may be difficult to keep up with the demands and quirks of a contract. Still, if you do not follow through on these items, the contract may not come to a successful completion, leaving you with a less-than-happy client. You may find that the client has lost confidence in your abilities and has chosen another agent to fulfill his real estate requirements going forward. The time and money that you invested in the first two parts of the business cycle is lost with no financial return.

Being good at one part of the cycle does not create success in the other areas. In fact, you may find that lack of skill in organizing the effective completion of the other two areas will spell your demise in the field of real estate sales. Remember, 80 percent of the business is completed by 20 percent of the agents. There is no secret that successful agents know and no pill they have taken that made them successful. It is simply the implementation of systems to handle the flow of the business in an orderly fashion, thus infusing clients with the confidence and excitement to be your cheerleaders, enthusiastically telling others of their marvelous experiences.

How Many Balls Can You Juggle?

A juggler can juggle one ball very well. Two balls seem easy, too. But when the third ball is added, a juggler needs skill and accuracy. And adding more takes great professionalism. Eventually, there are too many balls for any juggler to handle.

The same is true of real estate. You can only be doing so many things at once. Until you develop the systems to handle the variety of responsibilities that evolve for multiple transactions, you are limited to handling one, two, or maybe three transactions at a time.

Each transaction has several activities for which you are responsible. When you add to this the activities that you are responsible for coordinating, the number becomes immense. If you are trying to create more business, meet more clients face to face, and handle more transaction completion activities, the number is no longer immense: it is astronomical.

You can implement systems to handle more responsibilities simultaneously. You may need to have specialists in place to assist you. They may be already in place in your office. If you choose to expand your business to a higher level, then you may need to hire your own staff. Yet just hiring staff is not the answer. Systems must be in place at every level. The more effective the systems are at completing the assignment efficiently, the more you will be able to juggle.

A system is the implementation of a plan for handling each part of a task in the same manner each time that the task needs to be completed. Setting up a system means dividing the larger task into its component parts. Once it's divided up, a written plan identifies how to deal with each component.

Who will deal with it? What will they do? In what order will they do it? To whom will the completion of the task be reported, or how will there be a record of its completion?

Who will handle the next set of details, and how will they know that it is their turn to step up?

Establishing systems may seem tedious at first. If, however, the system is established appropriately, a temporary employee who has never worked for you can come in and know exactly what needs to be done, in what order, and by whom. When someone can do this by following written instructions, you have created a system.

Systems control the flow of tasks, prevent tasks from being missed or mishandled, and ensure the successful completion of the project. Less time is needed to complete tasks, because everyone knows what needs to be done and who is to do it. There is no lag time of analysis, assignment, and acrimony.

The Agent-Centered System

An agent-centered system is one in which everything is designed so that the agent is involved at every level. The object is to be sure that items are completed for the entire cycle. The agent is involved in these tasks, but there is a way of identifying the appropriate tasks, the sequence of their completion, and reporting the result.

The system permits the agent to be extremely effective in the completion of every phase. The agent can complete more transactions, because the systems eliminate the continuous series of mistakes and errors that occur in an unsystematic approach. Having a system is, therefore, better in every respect than the haphazard methods most agents use in the client identification, home-finding or home-selling experiences, and the processing of the transaction to closing.

Though better than an unsystematic method, it is still just as it is named: agent-centered. It requires the involvement of the agent at every level. If the agent is unavailable, sick, on vacation, or performing another task, the systems falter.

The Client-Centered System

The client-centered system places the agent on the periphery, not in the bull's-eye. As a result, the agent is not always required to complete a task. The systems may involve others who are on the agent's staff, the broker's staff, the loan officer's staff, the title company's staff, or vendors with whom the agent is comfortable working. In addition, forms of technological assistance can enable an agent-centered system.

These individuals and technologies can help to establish the system and add great strength to the agent's ability to handle more business with less personal time and effort. Doing more business with more time for personal growth opportunities becomes the key to generating healthier business practices, decreasing agent burnout, and enjoying a more meaningful personal life.

The key question to ask when establishing a client-centered system is, "What is the best way we can accomplish the task, keep the client well informed, and ensure the effective completion of this portion of the client event?"

Once the agent has selected the appropriate staff to assist in any system, the agent should invite them to sit and work through the establishment of the system together. No one person has all of the answers. Input from everyone involved will engage them in investing their time and effort into the procedure. Because they are involved in deciding the most appropriate way to handle the task, they feel a personal investment in the system. That high level of commitment enhances the efficacy of the system. Systems must be constantly reevaluated, because new requirements, ideas, and paperwork inevitably are injected into the process.

The Team Approach

Not everyone on a baseball team can be the pitcher. Ron Garber, a personal friend, taught me this principle. He helped me envision all of the members of the team playing the position in which they were most comfortable. Because everyone is playing their prime position, the team's play is smooth and professional. Each member of the team is working at peak proficiency with maximum comfort and minimum stress.

I have spoken predominantly of teams. You may be the agent who prefers to handle every assignment and fulfill every task. Solo agents are abundant in the real estate profession. Sometimes they work alone because of their high confidence level in their skills, other times because they are inexperienced at functioning with teams.

Working as a solo agent is limiting in terms of the hours and effort that you can put in during a day. It also does not permit a great deal of time off or personal time. The hands-on approach of the solo agent provides the client with one-on-one attention and a consistency of personality. It may, however, limit the amount of time that can be spent fulfilling the needs of each client. Advanced organizational skills are a must for the agent choosing the solo strategy.

Any solo agent will need a professional team of vendors for support. Outsourcing the parts of a transaction that do not need the agent's personalized attention is critical for time management. It is not easy to be in the office filing and processing listings and contracts and still be at appointments creating future opportunities.

One possibility in today's high-tech world is to work with virtual assistants. Virtual assistants work from their homes or another off-site location. Communication is generally via computer. They are contract help, not employees. You can hire these individuals for the number of hours required, paying by the hour or by the task completed. Avoiding employee relationships requires less management of one's support system. Many offices provide such assistance as in-office support. For example, brokers often provide nonemployee assistants on-site. The office in which I hold my license has this type of agent support for an enormous number of agents who choose to fly solo. The cost is based on a per-transaction or per-listing fee. The office takes care of employee concerns, wages, benefits, and payroll taxes. By using such staff, one can provide more extensive client care in a systematic and comfortable manner.

Each transaction, file, and client represents a large number of balls to juggle for the solo real estate professional. Multiply that by the number of clients being serviced, and the numbers can become mind boggling. Time-management systems are critical aspects of the single-agent business design.

I choose to be involved at the team level. I find that client service overall and the health of the agent are both improved by the team process. This arrangement takes planning, and decisions regarding the type of team members needed to staff a well-organized, client-oriented service framework, take careful consideration.

Peaks and Valleys

As we have discussed, real estate professionals can get bogged down in one portion of the business. Or we may become overwhelmed by an influx of business.

When that happens, the processing of the business will soon be the next problem. When we spend too much time in any one area, the other areas are neglected. The agent's organizational skills are typically the reason for such peaks and valleys.

But peaks and valleys can also come with seasonality (stronger surges in business during certain times of the year), worldwide financial swings (the fall of the stock market or a sudden change in interest rates), or world events or catastrophes that momentarily take center stage. Although not all of these events can be anticipated, we can have plans in place to deal with them when they occur.

Agents generally feel that the market slackens around Thanksgiving until after the New Year. Buyers and sellers are more involved with relatives than in changing homes. The spring market is a new season, especially in colder climates, when the snows melt and the flowers peek through the ground.

Interest rates are a matter of perception. If the public perceives the rate as high, they delay purchasing—unless rates look as though they will climb higher. In the early 80s, I was thrilled to receive a 12.5 percent interest rate for a new home. The next week, rates were 18 percent. The market slowed. Ronald Reagan declared that interest rates would reach single digits; there was a flurry of activity when it happened.

Be aware of interest rate directions. Know what they may do to the market. Watch market trends to gauge in advance the most likely direction of real estate sales. Prepare strategies to work in those markets. During peaks, the number of real estate agents swells tremendously. During valleys, the number of real estate agents diminishes due to many agents' lack of preparation.

4

Establishing a Business Plan

Beginning business planning for your real estate practice is the most important step anyone can take on the road to successful business development. Business planning is the road map that shows how an organization can reach a goal. If you have no destination in mind, you might arrive somewhere you didn't intend to be. A prepared real estate businessperson knows the ultimate destination and follows the plan set forth to get there.

A huge majority of agents do not have a written business plan. Those who do don't always follow it. Far fewer regularly review the plan to see if they are fulfilling it or if it needs minor (or major) adjustments for them to arrive at the defined destination.

In space travel, the slightest deviation from course means missing the destination by a huge distance. Business planning and follow-through are the same. In addition to formulating the initial plan, an entrepreneurial agent must revisit the plan and the current results to ensure that everything is moving towards the target.

What Do You Need as Income?

The first step in establishing a business plan is to identify the amount needed to fulfill your personal or family needs. What will be your living costs for the next 12 months? What must be set aside for savings? What must be invested for retirement (agents do not generally have a retirement program pre-established for them)? What amount must be set aside for future family goals like education and vacations? These amounts cannot be off-hand estimates. You must assess everything, from utility costs to insurance. You ought to know fairly precisely what your needs will be.

Once this number is firmly established, you must identify other income that is available to meet those needs. Can income from another person's employment be applied? Do you have residual income from employment in another field? Is steady income coming in from a trust? From rents? Because you are in the real estate business, you have the obligation and the opportunity to determine your standard of living.

The next step is simply to subtract the additional income available from the gross personal or family budget needed. All of these numbers must be precise and in writing. Approximations with no written format are not acceptable—they won't give your business the road map it needs to be successful.

Remember that the road to your destination will have turns in it. If you do not have written directions, you can easily make a wrong turn. Establish the amount needed for your personal or family financial life. Don't be stingy. Put down the dollars required for entertainment, savings, and charitable giving as well as clothing, food, mortgage payments, and utility bills.

To assist in identifying what should be included, a sample personal budget form has been included in the Appendix. Study it. Add to it. Put it on a spreadsheet so you can adjust it. Then live within the budget you create.

Having subtracted any alternative income amounts from the budget number, you have what we will refer to as the "net personal" or "family" requirement. Knowing this number is the first step in knowing what you must achieve through the real estate business to fund your life.

How Much Will the Business Cost to Run?

Now we move into the business budget. This is where you establish how much you are willing to spend in establishing and maintaining the business. You typically will pay some amount as you start your real estate career, because most real estate agents become members of the National Association of REALTORS®, state boards or associations of REALTORS®, local boards of REALTORS®, and local multiple-listing services (MLS).

There will be educational costs, too. Initially, you must fulfill your state's class and licensing requirements for agents and brokers, each with its requisite cost. Once in the field, continuing-education fees will be required on a periodic basis to maintain your license. In addition, you must get a professional education. The education required by most states familiarizes new agents with the laws and terms that you will need to know to function within the law and without losing your license. However, sales techniques, business planning, business technology, and how to interpret and adjust to changing markets are never covered in the licensing classes. This information is gained by attending other classes that are designed to enhance your professional skills.

Affiliation with an office or franchise may cost something. Signs, business cards, advertising, and support staff costs must be accounted for. A seasoned professional may be willing to share their budget with you. But you may find that even seasoned professionals do not prepare or follow a business budget. In a recent seminar with more than 200 seasoned agents attending, only 30 agents indicated that they had a written business budget, and only 10 indicated that they reviewed that budget more than once a year.

Many outside vendors, who want to sell you their product or idea, will try to expand your business budget. Having a written budget gives you the appropriate response if you are not convinced that their product or service will be a successful part of your business plan. You can always say to a vendor, "I establish my budget in November. Provide me with the information, and I will consider it when I review my budget for next year."

Not spending money on a whim will garner you considerable savings throughout your career. An extra few hundred dollars a month can add up to negative cash flow at the end of the year.

We have provided an example of a business budget in the Appendix. It is no more than a spreadsheet listing many of the categories necessary in a complete budget. You will need to adjust the budget categories based on your area, needs, and expenses.

What Is Your Target Market?

Another area that you must handle quickly in your business planning process is identifying those with whom you want to do business. It may seem presumptuous to identify a market if you are not already involved in the business, but it is critical for your business planning.

Will you "farm" (identify a geographic area to which you will market consistently), or will you cold call? Each approach has its own merits and its own set of expenses. If you are going to farm, then what price range do you want to cover? Covering several price ranges of homes by setting several different geographic areas to farm will help to adjust for changing markets. When the higher-priced homes are moving, the median or lower-priced homes may not be the main source of income. However, lower-priced homes tend to remain in demand longer. How often does the area you have identified turn over (how many homes come on the market and sell) each year? Does an agent already have a dominant share of that area? Is it appropriate to fight for that share, or would the cost and effort be better spent someplace else?

Some agents target senior buyers and sellers, emphasizing the growth of the baby boomers into this category. Others may target second home buyers, if the area has a large influx of those individuals. Still others target doctors, dentists, attorneys—people of a specific profession—because they feel that the average transaction will be higher and these people may invest in additional real estate. Each choice identifying or narrowing your target market helps to solidify decisions regarding advertising and client outreach. This in turn helps to clarify your business budget.

You may have more than one target market. You would do well to analyze geographic areas for their turnaround times, average sale price, percentage of homes that are on the market each year, and the percentage that actually sell. As mentioned previously, you will also want to analyze the history of the area to see what agent or agents are dominant there. If none seems to be dominant, it is an open market. If someone plays a very dominant role, then you must evaluate whether or not the area is worth the effort. One geographic area in which my partner and I chose to operate had two or three individuals with higher-than-average market shares, but the area was large enough and had enough turnover for us to move ahead. We are now the dominant force in an area of 3,700 homes. In a market of this size, being dominant can mean having just a few percentage points of the market. Smaller geographic markets tend to have higher percentage domination, just because there are fewer transactions. Your multiple-listing service should be your best source of information. Do the analysis so your decisions are founded in fact, not guesswork.

What Is the Average Sale Price in Your Target Market?

It is critical for you to know the price range for each market. As you fit more snugly into the framework of the target market, providing detailed information regarding the local housing market to your clients will help them perceive you as an expert. And as the expert in your target market, you will find more and more people turning to you for answers to their questions.

Knowing the price range for your market will also help you to estimate your potential income from working with that area, because potential income is derived from the sale price times your commission. Then you can project how much is worth spending on marketing to that target. This begins your evaluation of dollars returned per dollars spent, which will help you to know where best to spend your hard-earned money.

What Average Net Commission Percentage Will You Earn?

Your net commission percentage depends on your negotiation skills with the seller, in the case of a listing, and with the buyer, if you are performing under a buyer-agency agreement. The commission is either the percentage you agree to take of the sales price or the amount offered by a co-op broker. Additionally, you may work as the buyer's agent and determine ahead of time the minimum percentage of the sales price or the fixed minimum amount you will accept. This agreement should always be in writing. You know what percentage for which you are willing to work, and you know what listing agents offer through the multiple-listing service for your cooperation in bringing them a buyer.

This percentage will be adjusted by your arrangement with your broker. Some brokers are on a 50/50 split basis. Those working on teams will also be on a split basis. You may work for a company that has a 100 percent program. You need to decide up front what you are willing to work for and how much you are willing to spend to receive that percentage. Some brokers who provide splits also provide significant help in covering what would otherwise be your overhead. Teams work in this same fashion. In a 100 percent program, however, you are required to provide all of the overhead and a profit margin for the broker.

Once you determine your average percentage per transaction and then modify that amount by whatever split you are on, you must consider whether you will have to pay a referral fee. If another agent sent you the transaction, that agent will usually expect a part of the commission as a reward for providing you with the business.

When you have accounted for all of these figures, you will have a sense of your average net commission percentage. Then you can use this figure to ascertain your average commission per transaction.

What Is the Average Commission per Transaction?

Now that you know the average sale price per transaction and the average transaction net commission percentage, you can calculate the average commission per transaction. You may wonder why this number is significant. This figure tells you how many transactions you need to generate the amount of gross commission income in your business budget.

Knowing the average sale price and the average net commission percentage gives you the average commission you will receive per transaction: simply multiply one by the other to generate the answer.

How Many Transactions Must You Close to Earn Your Target Income?

Once again, this is simply a matter of math. Once you have decided on your target income (by adding your personal net budget to the business budget), divide that by your average commission income per transaction. The result is the number of transactions you must achieve.

With this method, you have a systematic way of identifying in advance your target number of transactions per year. With that goal on paper, you can create an effective business plan to close that many transactions.

As you adjust your target marketing, the average sale price, and your average net commission percentage, you adjust your average commission per transaction. This in turn adjusts the number of transactions required to achieve the target amount.

To make this figure accurate on an ongoing basis, you must keep track of the statistics. You need to know the sale price of every transaction and the average commission percentage. Then you can calculate an accurate average commission based on a valid history. Ultimately, you will see that this approach not only provides you with statistical information to plan for the future but also gives you valid statistics from which to base the valuation of the asset you are developing—a real estate business.

How Many Transactions Will Be Sold Listings?

You may wonder why it is important for you to plan how many of your transactions will be sold listings. As a part of your business plan, you must know whether you are targeting sellers or buyers. You should know how many of each you will need to fulfill the business plan.

You can use the shotgun approach, meaning that your marketing is scattered looking for any buyer or seller. With this approach, you do not have a target in mind for the type of transaction you will be eliciting from the public. You can choose to target the transactions, meaning that you have defined your potential clients, the geographic area you want to do business in, and the price range with which you want to work. Your interest in various geographic areas or groups will determine how you market since each will require a different approach.

Knowing how many listings sold you need also sets you up to know other aspects of your listing business. There is a logical sequence of knowledge that will lead you to understand and plan your business.

How Many of the Listings Will Sell?

Typically, not every listing taken turns into a listing sold. You need to understand the statistics of your area. In the MLS, how many of the listings are actually selling in the current market? (For those new to the industry, the multiple-listing service is the cooperative effort among brokers to provide information on their listings. This is typically sponsored by the local Association of REALTORS®. Members provide their information on listings and their offer to compensate other agents for selling their listings. It is the repository for a great deal of significant information on the local market.) This statistic changes in different market conditions. When the market is tight and fewer listings are available, perhaps 95 percent sell during their initial listing period. In a flat market, however, that figure may be less than 30 percent.

Knowing the statistical data for your area and for the current market is critical. Keeping an eye on the market on a regular basis is important, too, or else the market will change, but you will be unaware. Are 100 homes coming on the market each day? Are 30 showing as sold each day? How are you dealing with an increase of 70 homes a day in your market availability? Or are 20 homes a day coming on the market, and 25 showing up sold each day? How are you dealing with the scarcity of available listings?

Each change in the market modifies your business plan. The business runs in cycles. You can assume that the constant dynamic in real estate is change. The market will be different next year from this year. Once you have gone through several cycles, you will understand the process. If you anticipate market modifications, you will not have to wait for cycles to repeat to understand what they mean.

The typical cycle has a tight market segment, in which just not enough inventory is available for sale. Prices move upward at an unusual pace. Most homes receive multiple offers. Selling time frames are short. Prices may go well above list price. This part of the cycle is referred to as a *seller's market.*

Eventually, buyers slow down, either because of a large increase in pricing or because of an economic change in the area (loss of many jobs or significant financial changes in the public arena). It will be some time before buyers move back into the market as intensely. Now, there are more listings than buyers. Inventory swells, and prices flatten. This part of the cycle is referred to as a *buyer's market.* Buyers have more choices, and the offer process has room for negotiation. These market types last from a few days or weeks to months or even over a year.

Eventually, the available inventory of homes and the number of buyers evens out. Marketing time frames level off. Prices are more consistent and predictable. Some refer to this part of the cycle as a "normal" real estate market. In real estate, however, there is no such thing as a normal market; it is, rather, an *even market*. It no longer favors buyers or sellers.

How Many Appointments Do You Need to Go On Before You Are Selected as the Listing Agent?

What is your success rate for converting appointments into listings? How many other agents are being called in to give a presentation? How effective is your presentation? Do you sign nine out of every ten sellers to whom you present your information? Do you sign six out of ten? Do you struggle to sign one out of ten?

Your ability to convert appointments into listings is an important piece of your business plan. What information do you take into the appointment? How do you present it? Do you know the statistics for the area, or do you just wing it? Your skill, confidence, and knowledge will show. As you increase your levels of professionalism in each area, you will increase your percentages. Again, that will become a key feature of your business plan.

Providing a consistent picture of what you do, your results, and your team or organization setup can be accomplished through providing a prelisting package. This is the professional-looking printed material that answers most of a potential seller's questions before your meeting. Providing this material up front shortens your appointment time, increases your conversion ratio, and inspires a greater level of confidence in your professional skills.

Classes and tapes are available that can help you develop outstanding prelisting materials. In addition, the organization of your actual presentation will give strength to your professional image. Plan it well. Have it look as professional as possible (including printing your material in color). Your attention to preparation and systematic approach when making the presentation will increase your success ratio in gaining prospects as clients.

Putting It All Together

Your conversion ratio will help your business planning. To meet your annual target number of listings sold, you need to know how many listing appointments you must go on each year, each month, and each week.

The formula is simple: if you need 24 listings sold to meet your business plan, and 6 out of every 10 listings in the MLS are selling in your current market, then dividing 24 by 0.6 results in 40 listings. In that case, you must list 40 properties to meet your business plan. If you get 8 listings out of every 10 appointments, then divide 40 listings by 0.8 to get 50, and you need to go on at least 50 listing appointments to meet your business plan. That translates to a minimum of four to five listing appointments a month, or approximately one every week, to meet your goal. If, on the other hand, you get only 5 listings for every 10 listing appointments, then 40 listings divided by 0.5 is 80, and you must go on 80 listing appointments a year, or 6 to 7 appointments a month, to get your 40 listings.

Any of these scenarios should lead to 2 listings sold every month. Because your target for this part of your business plan is 24 listings sold for the year, at a rate of 2 listings sold per month, you will achieve your goal.

How Many of the Transactions Will Be Buyer Sales?

If you know the total number of transactions you need to close to meet your income goal, and you know how many listings sold you intend to have, then you also know how many of the remaining transactions you must complete by representing buyers. Working with buyers will involve an entirely different skill set.

It is imperative that your business plan has a design for acquiring buyer leads. They may come through your listings by virtue of signs and brochures on the listings. Buyer leads could also come from ads that you place in papers, magazines, and the Internet. Also, your database of past clients will provide you with leads if you stay in touch with them and ask for their assistance. All of these methods can provide transactions of either variety, but you must prepare yourself through your business plan to meet the needs of buyers as well as sellers.

Hone your skills with buyers. Knowing your market well will show through in your interaction with them. Your ability to answer questions regarding the community, schools, parks and the workings of the park district, programs within the community, places of worship, health facilities, lenders, the buying process, and the types of homes available within the market will instill confidence in your buyers. The higher the level of confidence that you create with your potential buyers, the more buyers will consummate a purchase through your efforts.

Just as you will have a conversion ratio of the number of listing appointments to create a certain number of listings, you will create a conversion ratio with potential buyers. Some will buy from you. Some will go to another agent. Will 5 out of 10 of your buyer leads become part of your client list? Maybe 8 of every 10 will purchase a home from you. That conversion rate tells you how many buyers you need to work with to achieve the number of buyer sales in your business plan. The formula is the same one used with listings: take the number of buyer transactions you need to close and divide it by the percentage of conversions you have with buyers.

5

The Calendar and Your Business Plan

Real estate agents tend to become very involved in the day-to-day tasks of their practices. They see today's obligations but fail to see the larger picture and do what's needed to maintain a constant flow of future business. A calendar can assist the agent in focusing on the bigger picture. Today's appointment with a buyer is important, but if you forget to advertise your listing when you promised a seller you would, you may be losing one client while fulfilling another's needs. Once you plan out events, you will find that your real estate business is orderly, organized, and optimally successful.

Using the calendar will force you to think through your business plan and identify when tasks will be done. How many times a year will you send mailings to your past client database and sphere of influence: once a month, once every two months, or once a year? Your effectiveness may depend on the frequency and type of contact.

Will you send out a newsletter? Will you send postcards? Will you need to use a mailing service? Will you communicate via e-mail; if so, how will you get the e-mail addresses?

How will you get the physical addresses if mail is to go that route? How long will it take to set up the project? Who will prepare the material to be sent out, and how long before creating it must design and information be available? If the material will be printed, how much lead time does the printer need?

The skill you develop at using the calendar will save you from the "oh, I forgot" syndrome. Once calendared, events will flow in sequence, creating business at an even pace.

The calendar is not chiseled into a rock. It is a flexible but predetermined schedule of events. Some deadlines, such as dates for your advertisements, must be considered well ahead of time. You need to decide where and how often you are advertising. Working without a calendar is essentially saying that you are working without a business plan—in effect, that a business plan is unnecessary.

After years of functioning in the real estate field without calendaring events, let me tell you that the world changes when you fully plan your business design and schedule your success. You no longer find yourself rushing around on the day the ad is due or an hour before the event, making last-minute dashes to pick up supplies that should have been in place days before.

Big Rocks

Stephen Covey and others tell the story of a professor who walks into a classroom and sets up the materials for his lesson. A large glass cylinder is set on the table at the front of the room. The professor takes a bucket of fist-size rocks and places them carefully into the cylinder until no more rocks can fit.

At this point, he asks the class if the cylinder is full. Several students say yes.

He raises a bucket of pebbles and begins to pour the pebbles into the cylinder. These smaller rocks slide down among the larger rocks, and he can place quite a number into the cylinder. Finally, no more pebbles will fit.

He then asks the class to tell him if the cylinder is full. Heads bob up and down.

After this, the professor raises a bucket of sand above the desk at the front of the room. He proceeds to pour the sand into the glass container until there is no more room. One more time, he raises the question: Is the container full? The students are not certain what could possibly be added to this container, yet they are reticent to give an answer.

Once again a bucket is retrieved from the floor. This time it contains water. The professor pours until he is certain that adding another drop would cause the container to overflow.

Is the container full? The question seems to have only one answer. "Yes," come the replies. It is now full.

The professor steps back and asks the class to explain to him what they have learned from the demonstration. Timidly, one student responds that you can put more into life than you ever dreamed possible. The professor smiles slightly and tells the student that though the answer is true, it is not the one for which he was searching.

When no other responses are forthcoming, the professor tells the class the truth he wants them to learn. "If you don't put in the big rocks first, they will never fit."

What are your big rocks? What do you want to accomplish most in your lifetime? Where would you like to visit before you leave the planet? Is there a mountain you want to climb? Is there a book you would like to write? Are there books you would like to read? Do you have loved ones you have not visited, spoken with, communicated with in a long time? Do some of them live in your house? Are there friends from your past with whom you have'nt had contact for years?

Would you like to have a massage once a week? Do you want to get into shape? Is there a language you would like to learn? Are there ten languages you would like to learn? Do you want to paint or draw or take photos? Would you like to sculpt or carve or create a magnificent piece of furniture? Would you like to build a house? Do you want to take classes that you thought were too frivolous? Is there a car you would like to own and drive?

Many of us have never taken the time to write a list of the big rocks we want in life. Some are simple. You may want to take a walk with your child. You may want to read a book every night with your friend. You may want your family to go on a cruise together.

Big rocks do not have to be earth shattering. They should be things that would make you extraordinarily happy. A big rock is something that, once you have achieved it, will make you glow inside.

You may be saying to yourself, "I thought this was a book about my real estate career." It is. You simply need to understand that real estate sales is not your life. It is simply a marvelous way to fund your life. You are and will always be more than your real estate career.

We are talking about calendars. The calendar is like the glass container. As you place all of the items into your calendar, you will see it fill to the brim with events, to-dos, and I-musts. I would like to challenge you as a part of your life plan to make a list of a hundred big rocks. Some will take a lot of time and money. Others will take little of either. Once you have the list, or even a partial list, I want you to search the calendar and begin to place several of them throughout the days of this next year.

Put the big rocks in ahead of everything else. You do not need to accomplish all of them this year. You have a lifetime ahead of you. As you create the asset of a real estate practice, you will find that some big rocks that seemed potentially unattainable will find their way into your plan. I have visited New Zealand with my daughter, and we drove through the countryside for nearly three weeks. I have taken a trip to Australia with my son and spent two weeks absorbing the culture and the people with him. I visited Bali, where I stayed in the Ritz Carlton and had breakfast each morning overlooking the Indian Ocean, awakened each morning by the fragrances of flowers. When one of my sons decided he wanted to study for three months in London, he and I headed for England. I helped him get acclimated before I left him, a teenager, on his own in a foreign country.

Once, I would not have dreamed any of it was possible. However, when I determined how my career would fund my dreams and the dreams of my beloved family and friends, real estate became the most marvelous opportunity that I could have imagined. It is not just a career; it is the means of financing my big rocks.

Place your big rocks in first. Otherwise, they won't fit into your busy schedule. Life will fill up, and in the end, it will not be what it is meant to be. In my faith, a phrase is heard often: "Man is that he might have joy." Please find your joy.

Backdate Your Calendar

Putting the events that are important to you on your calendar requires a skill that I refer to as "backdating." Let's say that a newsletter needs to go out monthly. What date every month will it go out? Whatever date you choose, be consistent; it should go out on the same day every month. To get it out on this day, what needs to get done? If the newsletter is being mailed, then it must be labeled. How many days prior to the send date is the labeling date? Every month, the labeling date needs to be on the calendar. Then how much time before labeling will it need to be printed? Place that date on your calendar, too. How many days before printing must the newsletter be created so that it can be printed? Do real estate topics need to be chosen and articles written? Is there design work to be done? Will pictures need to be taken? Move back from the date of the ultimate event to calendar all of its parts so that whoever is going to accomplish them knows what to do well in advance. This is the process of backdating.

If the event is a "big rock," then you need to know when the event will occur. If it involves traveling, you may need to book airline tickets. Typically, the earlier they are booked, the less expensive they are and the more likely you'll get your preferred schedule. Do you need hotel reservations? Must tickets for a play or athletic event be acquired? Who will handle your real estate clients while you are gone? When every event in your world is backdated on your calendar, you will find that life flows at a much more even pace with few hassles.

The "Task Master"

The "Task Master" is a form designed to organize your tasks. Basically, it is a three-page organizer that breaks down the main tasks into subtasks. It provides a place for due dates and to indicate who will be in charge of accomplishing or leading the accomplishment of that task. In your real estate business plan, you will find that using the "Task Master" will facilitate your thought process.

Page one is a place to list the tasks that need to be accomplished. You may have 3 tasks or you may have 20 tasks that have to be addressed. Collect the description of each of these items on page one of the Task Master. The more tasks you decide need to be accomplished, the more organized your life will become. From advertising to training your staff, from buying a moving van to putting together a vendor list, from marketing to a target group of investors to writing real estate articles for the newspaper, this will focus you on your short- and long-term responsibilities.

Page two deals with each of the designated tasks on page one. There is a page two for every one of those tasks. If you have 20 items on page one (or series of page ones), then you have 20 copies of page two. On page two, the larger task is described. At this point, the person or persons who are heading up this task are named and the date of accomplishment is reiterated. The rest of each page two creates the subtasks necessary to accomplish the main task.

For example, one of your main tasks may be to have a client party. The date for the party will be designated on page one and transferred to the page two for this task. The subtasks are then delineated. Invitations will need to be sent out. The place of the party needs to be reserved. The theme needs to be identified. Entertainment must be secured. The food needs to be arranged for. The physical logistics must be prepared for the guests. Decorations need to be planned and put up. Clean up and trash control are essential, too.

Stating the date by when each subtask needs to be accomplished is critical. For example, the party's theme and location must be identified before the invitations go out so the invitations have meaningful information on them.

There must be a page three for each of the subtasks. The invitations, for example, must have all of the pertinent information identified. You must determine how many times invitations will be sent to the target audience. Generally, a single invitation for this type of event is insufficient to obtain maximum attendance. Also, you must identify an appropriate style and content for the invitations. Will they be postcards, letters, or brochures? What graphics will be required? When will each invitation be sent out? Therefore, by what date will each need to be prepared? By when will they need to be printed? How will you address or label them? Where will you get the list of invitees from? Will the invitations go out through e-mail or by U.S. Postal Service? Who will be in charge of each of these smaller tasks? Page three for each main subtask shows what will be handled by what date and by whom.

Page four is a flow chart that indicates how these three pages work together. It is designed to help you see the larger picture. If you use the format that we have provided in the Appendix, you will find the organization of your tasks much easier. Your calendar will receive all this information so that the larger picture of how the event is being organized is in plain view.

Scheduling Your Business Budget

As you look at your calendar and begin to identify what will happen during the year, you will be able to insert the amounts to be spent on each activity into your business budget. By using the calendar, you are placing the items that will need to be paid for on a time line showing when the money will be due. This time line will assist you in determining the number of closings required to meet these financial needs.

By using this planning mechanism, you preplan your expenses. You will not be lured into spending money on an item that is not in the budget, unless you are fully convinced that the item will enhance your business. All through the year, vendors will try to convince you to spend money on their form of advertising or lead generation. By keeping your calendar in front of you, you can decide if changing your real estate business plan is justified. Certainly, the calendar will not hold all of your expenses, but it will be a guideline for many major expenses. For example, are you going to a conference or educational seminar? When is your registration due? Will you need to make travel and hotel reservations? Being out of town will preclude you from being involved in some other areas of the business during that time. You may need to have a team member or another agent in your office handle these items. Have you made those arrangements in time? Will there be a cost to having someone else substitute for you? Will closings need to be attended? Inspections conducted? Clients who will need assistance?

As you become more at ease with using the calendar to organize your business schedule and budget, you will find a sense of peace. Knowing what is ahead and what needs to be done in a timely manner provides freedom. This freedom will translate into a better bottom line and a growth mode that fits your business plan.

6

The Business Budget

A detailed business budget will help you know the state of your business at all times. Before you spend a penny, you should organize your business plan according to its scheduled budget. Budgets are spending plans put together in advance of the actual expenditures; they are not the accumulation of information about what you have already spent. That is referred to as accounting. You will perform accounting tasks, which, when compared with your budget, will tell you where you stand vis-á-vis your business plan.

Your preplanning of activities and their cost is the key to your continued success in real estate sales. If you do not know how much you are spending or should spend, then you are simply hoping for a real estate career instead of planning one. Consistent reviews, too, will help you to stay on track. If the market is shifting and you find that you need to adjust your plan, a budget allows you to do so with confidence that you are in control of your business. Your business is not in control of you.

Retain a professional financial counselor, such as an accountant who can meet with you monthly to review your expenditures. This review through someone else's eyes can be very revealing and will be worth every dollar spent. The accountant may make suggestions that you might not otherwise put into place. Some will be tax-saving procedures. Others will help you to put money away for retirement. Others will simply be good investment advice.

The Calendar Will Serve As Your Reason to Say "No."

There will always be someone who is sure that if you give them your money, your business will flourish. Salespeople are typically the most daunted by saying no to other salespeople.

You need to analyze the potential of any investment in your business plan. Has another agent used this approach? What were the results? What is the dollar return per dollar invested? If the ratio is one to one or two to one, you may not want to consider changing your plan. If the approach consistently delivers a ten-to-one return for other agents, however, then I advise you to consider it strongly.

The one caveat is that you need to talk with the agents who have used the item or method and not just take the vendor's word. Amazingly, those trying to sell you something may report overly dramatic results. Real estate agents who are true professionals are willing to share their experience honestly. Be sure that the agent who is using the item, product, or service is not receiving money, discounts, or other rewards for their endorsement.

The dialogue that you should use consistently with vendors is, "I complete my budget for the year in November. Provide me with the information, and I will consider it as I prepare for next year." You will likely never hear from them again. There are few new or unique real estate advertising opportunities. Be sure that you want to spend the money; don't say yes without doing research first.

I believe that we have a responsibility to give to charitable organizations. I do not, however, think you must give just because you are asked. I tell charitable organizations to submit their requests and that I make my decisions in November for the following year. Decide in advance how much money you will budget for charity and then distribute that amount appropriately. Be sure to determine what impact your donation can have. We provide a scholarship for the Hispanic Chamber of Commerce. This shows up in our growing home sales within the Hispanic community.

It is amazing: when you do not have a logical response in place, those who want your money persist in attempting to achieve their goal, not yours. When you have things organized and give a logical answer, however, you may not have to say, "What part of *no* do you not understand?" Planning with your calendar in hand will make your real estate business much easier to manage.

What Determines the Reason for "Yes"?

You can say yes to offers of a project or product, when it fits within the parameters of your business plan and the return ratio likely will be high. You don't say yes off the cuff with no planning, however. Don't get caught up in hype. Be realistic about the potential return. Talk with agents who have already used the product or technique. Find out how long they have used it, how long before they saw a return, and if they have made it a permanent part of their budget and business plan. You do not have to be the first in line for every innovation in real estate marketing. You need to see consistency in your current real estate business design before adding to it. Be sure that you are implementing your current business design before adding another print ad, Web site, or blogging site to the list.

Yes is an important word. It seems to cost money every time you use it. Use it sparingly and with great thought. Do not omit it from your vocabulary, but use it with the respect it deserves.

Dollar-Productive Activities

Dollar-productive activities are those events that actually create cash flow. For the licensed agent, it is being eyeball-to-eyeball with a buyer or seller. It is listing a house. It is negotiating a contract. It is finalizing a transaction.

How much are you worth per hour? Attorneys, psychiatrists, physicians, and others place their hourly rates at hundreds of dollars per hour. If you use the normal 2,000 hours per year for a full-time business, then if you are grossing $250,000 per year, you are worth $125 per hour. Raise your gross, and your time is worth much more. Would you pay someone $100 per hour to put up signs? What would you pay for stuffing envelopes?

For a licensed agent, licking envelopes after stuffing them is not a dollar-productive activity. Putting up a sign can be hired out. Performing everyday tasks, as necessary as they are, takes time away from the main focus of your business. Listing, selling, and negotiating are how you earn a living.

Design your days so that you are involved as much as possible in income-producing activities. Plan your business so that others can support you. When you find yourself involved in non-dollar-productive activities, then you need to adjust your business plan.

An "hour of power" is time set aside to make prospecting phone calls to potential buyers, sellers, or individuals who will refer buyers or sellers to you. It can be programmed into your schedule. Philadephia's Allan Domb, declared by the National Association of REALTORS® (NAR) to be the top real estate agent in the United States, is involved with a hundred phone calls every day. While he finishes with one call, an assistant is dialing his next call. The assistant listens in and takes notes of what needs to be done and makes sure those items are completed. Allan's commitment to contacting his sphere of influence and his leads makes him the number-one agent in the country. He knows what dollar productivity is and uses that concept to his benefit.

Dollar-productive activity is the essence of the day's activities for agents who are serious about their business. Coffee klatches with the rest of the agents in the office are not a required part of the day, but doing business is. Make a list of things that you can do to create cash flow and schedule them into your day. Create an outline of the perfect day in your business, and make it the basis for how you structure each of your days. You will have no problem deciding what activities are dollar-productive.

Lead Sources

What are the sources of your business? Do you know where it comes from? If you have no idea where your business comes from, then how do you decide where to spend your money?

Some sources are obvious. Buyers call when they see For Sale signs. When you have informational brochures in a box attached to the sign, they may become more intrigued about the home. If you have a list of the other homes you have available with basic information about them on the back of the flier, then even if they aren't interested in that home, they may call about one of the others. Future sellers also pick up these fliers and note your signs. They want to know how you market the homes you have listed.

You may want to send out postcards to the community when you list a home nearby and again when it sells. This marketing tactic keeps your name on potential customers' minds and provides relevant information. Your activity in their area may very well spur them to call you when they are ready to buy or sell. They'll tell you, "I see that you do a lot of business in our area."

The Internet has become quite an active source of business for real estate agents. Pictures and information about the homes you have listed are important to potential buyers and sellers. You will find that the average buyer has researched online and developed a sense of what properties are available.

You need to have the type of Web site to which buyers and sellers will want to return. It must be easy to use and replete with pictures and information. Have in place an automatic follow-up system, so that your potential clients feel that you care about them and are consistently in touch with them.

If your MLS system does not have an automatic procedure for updating your clients, then you may need to find another commercial system that does. When you input that individual's parameters, then every new listing that comes up is e-mailed to them. You can use this technology with buyers or sellers. Potential sellers like to keep in touch with the market, so they can see trends as they prepare their homes for sale. Buyers like to know about each home that comes on the market, and this use of e-mail can notify them within seconds of a home's being put into the MLS.

Keep in touch with your past clients. They can become your advocates. They simply need to be reminded that you would like them to be watching out for you. They ought to have an idea of what to say and how to get others to contact you. In response, a letter updating them on the progress of clients they refer is a nice touch. It might even be nice to take the two groups to dinner at your expense.

It is common knowledge that most real estate agents do not stay in touch with past customers. NAR indicates that after two years, a full 80 percent of buyers do not remember from whom they purchased their home. If their agents had stayed in touch, then there would be no question. You need to stay in touch with regular mailings or e-mails. A newsletter is another possibility.

If you have your prospective clients fill out an information form, then you can get their e-mail address. You may also ask for the names, addresses, birthdays, and other key information about other members of the household. If you are using a database designed around sales, then you can have these dates appear on your scheduler. Birthday cards can be created inexpensively on today's computers and printers. You can also create animated e-mails for special events. Every contact with these people will remind them of who you are and the role you played in their lives.

"Orphans" is the term for another agent's clients who have either purchased your listing or whose listing your client has purchased. They are referred to as orphans in anticipation that the other agent will not stay in touch. Sometimes after receiving your materials for a while, they may believe that you were the one who assisted them in their purchase or sale. If you know that the other agent is efficient and will contact them, however, then you may decide not to pursue that client.

One of the surest ways to remind your clients of the role that you played in their lives is to sponsor a client party. In Illinois, I sponsored a party that was more formal, involving the adults. In Arizona, we sponsor a more casual party where clients can bring their children. We hold it in a park where there are swings and playground equipment, and we buy food and host jumping castles, a balloon artist, and inflated obstacle courses. Soon afterward, we seem to receive many client referrals from those who were invited. Not all invitees come each year, but they don't want to be forgotten. We send three invitations to the event about three weeks apart with the final invitation coming the week of the event. It is amazing how many people forget about an event without a last-minute reminder.

Advertising in print media is often ineffective. Newspaper ads may bring in some business, but they are the least productive form of advertising in terms of dollar spent per dollar received. Real estate magazines seem to draw clients more heavily than newspapers. Some agents do no print advertising. Bob Wolff, one of the top agents in the United States, has not done any print advertising. His campaigns are all centered around past clients and his sphere of influence. Month after month, he sends letters to these people with a personalized note. He sends out copies of articles that his staff finds featuring news in the lives of friends, clients, and acquaintances. As he sends a copy for their files, he jots a personal note to let them know that he cares. His method is absolutely effective. His constant flow of buyers and sellers can be traced directly to his constant communication.

Another major source of business can be other agents. When I worked in Illinois, a full 20 percent of my business came from agent referrals. Typically a referral fee is paid to the referring broker, and it ranges most often from 20 to 30 percent, with 25 percent being the most common. Marketing to other agents from around the country and the world takes determined effort. If you have a designation, such as Certified Residential Specialist (CRS), then you may market to the members of that organization. If you belong to a franchise, then you may market to the franchise for business. Agents tend to be loyal to those who are similar to themselves. I have had a personal promotion booth at the convention for the franchise with which I am affiliated every year since 1985. It has brought a tremendous return—at least ten to one—on the time, effort, and dollars invested.

Every source of business ought to be thoroughly considered. What will each cost? What kind of effort will it take?

What will be the return on investment? Keeping track of the leads derived from your sources takes additional effort, but it's the only way to determine if the investment has been worthwhile. Without considering leads alongside their source, you may continue to attempt to derive business from sources that cost more than they earn. We have included an example in the Appendix of a simple way to keep track of your leads. There is also a form for contracts written and contracts closed that includes a place to indicate the source of the buyer or seller. By using these forms, you can determine how many leads from a particular source actually turn into transactions.

7

How You Organize Your Business Will Determine Your Success

Organizing your business properly from day one will save significant time, money, and confusion. Analyzing your business on a constant basis is essential for its control and growth. Many areas must be considered in the organizational design.

The business flow of which we spoke earlier is the center of the planning process. It is important to identify the methods you will choose to handle each phase of the business. As you determine the design, you will find peace of mind knowing that the systems will handle the flow of business without disruption.

Organizing Your Staff

Your long-term vision for your business sets the parameters for hiring staff. Do you want to hire in-house staff, or do you want to pay vendors? Does your broker provide staff for a fee? Each of these designs leads to different systems to handle the real estate flow.

If you envision yourself as the person always meeting clients, then the design of your business will focus on keeping you in that dollar-productive position. If you envision yourself as the CEO of your real estate business, then you will design a system in which other members of your team are one–on-one with the clients.

You need to decide when in your career you will need others to take over the parts of the business that you no longer have the time or the will to accomplish efficiently. For instance, a listing coordinator can process all of the paperwork, input listings to the MLS, keep in touch with sellers, and prepare and complete advertising. A closing coordinator can take all contracts from acceptance through closing. This person will stay in touch with the parties involved (buyer or seller, other agent, lender, title company, and, in some states, an attorney) to make sure that all of the tasks involved in the transaction are accomplished according to the required dates and times in the contract..

As your leads increase, you may need to have licensed assistants who can work directly with the buyers and sellers. On some teams, these individuals are restricted to working with either buyers or sellers. On other teams, they are available to work with both.

The stronger the licensed personnel, the stronger the administrative personnel need to be. You may move from a personal production of 60 transactions a year to a team production of several hundred transactions each year. As you potentially transition from being the out-front agent to CEO, you will need to empower your team members to fulfill their assignments without your direct supervision.

Giving up some control requires having confidence in the individuals in administrative positions. That's why it is necessary to prepare detailed job descriptions for each position. Also, each team member should be cross-trained for all of the other positions on the team. Should someone be out sick for a week, who can handle their work so that the team does not falter? Should someone choose to leave the team, who can step in and train the replacement? When cross-trained staff is in place, no individual can hold you hostage by threatening to leave. No one is indispensable.

Of course, you should spend time getting to know and understand your staff. Having a good working relationship with each team member is critical, and the staff should function amicably when working together. In addition, the longer you maintain good staff, the better the team functions. The experience of competent staff members who are positive about the team bolsters team spirit.

It is just as important that you have confidence in those who are licensed assistants. They work with your clients and develop relationships that can lead to other referrals or repeat business. The allegiance of these clients needs to be formed towards the team, not just the individual handling the lead. Communication from you is important to maintain their loyalty. The client party is a great way for these people to get to know you. You also need to involve a variety of team members throughout the transaction so that the clients see the advantage of the team approach. Each contact should be designed with this intent.

How Will You Organize Your Database?

Your database is the information about those with whom you will maintain contact throughout your real estate career. These are the individuals who will do business with you again or who will send others to do business with you, including clients, vendors, and other agents. A good database has accurate phone numbers, fax numbers, e-mail addresses, mailing addresses, addresses of property owned by these people, and a history of your relationship with them through notes and comments. Remember to list family members, birthdays, and anniversaries as well as the dates when these individuals purchased or sold real estate.

The data must be current. You need to stay in touch with people in the database so that you will know if their information has changed. Your consistent communication with this group will increase their confidence in you. They will know that you care and that you remember who they are. As mentioned previously, after two years, 80 percent of buyers do not remember from whom they purchased a home. If your communication with past clients and your sphere of influence is strong and consistent, then they will not suddenly develop amnesia when friends, relatives, and acquaintances ask for a reference to the agent who sold them their home.

Control of your data is significant for many reasons. Right now, you need to know with whom you are doing business. Your database will contain names of prospects, clients, past clients, your sphere of influence, and vendors. This is the place to go when you need to get in touch with one or all of them.

Software can make the job either easier—or harder. You need a database system that is available when you need it. Another concern is how well it will keep you informed of tasks related to your contacts. How often do you need to send out letters? When are their birthdays? Alongside the tasks of showing homes, listing homes, and negotiating contracts, does the software or Webware keep you up to date on your pending tasks and when they need to be completed? Will it store the information for the long term so that you can keep in touch with contacts over the years? Will it keep records of what you have done to keep in touch with them? Will you be able to pull a list of people to invite to your client appreciation party? Can the software divide people up according to which team member worked with them? Can it divide the names according to farm areas or other categories? Each task it can perform will ease your load, make you more efficient, and return greater response from prospects.

One effective database program is the Web-based program Top Producer. It offers the flexibility of entering your database from any computer in the world. For a solo agent, this product provides the most latitude in controlling and using the database directly. There are software-based versions of Top Producer, and there are multiple user systems so that your entire team can be tied into the same database, essential for team coordination.

Another system is Agent Office, solely a software-based system. It is the system that has been networkable for the longest period of time for the real estate community. It requires a computer or server that is accessible through other means (GoToMyPC.com or another comparable service) or by employing a third party to supply the service to make the information accessible from any computer.

A newer real estate specific netware called 360 Agent has been developed by the same individuals who created Agent Office. It provides a Web-based service with the same features and ease of use as Agent Office but with a more extensive business planning and monitoring function.

New versions of current database systems will be created on a regular basis. New technology will undoubtedly create new database systems with intensified power and adaptability to newly identified needs.

Keeping Track of Income and Expenses

A real estate businessperson must always know how much money is needed to pay the bills, how much is profit, which investments leverage a high return, and the projection of future needs. Far too many agents have no idea what their cost is of doing business, but successful real estate agents know and understand their income and expenses.

QuickBooks is the most dominant piece of software used by real estate agents. Such software may require an expert to visit your office for setup. More complex systems that can provide even greater flexibility in reporting, such as Peachtree, are available but require even more training and management skills as well as a greater initial monetary investment.

Look at reports of your spending in each category of your business on a monthly basis. Compare those figures to your budget. Look at both the amounts for the month and the total spent year to date. You may be way under early in the year for client entertainment, but that will change if you hold a party next month. It is important to tie your planning calendar to your expenses so you have a timely indication of the amount spent in each area. QuickBooks can prepare and print the reports that you need to make these comparisons. You want to perform this same comparison on an annual basis, as you compile numbers that will be used in valuating your business. Comparison of these numbers from year to year will chart your progress in business planning, placing you far ahead of the majority of real estate agents.

You must start with a budget in mind. If you do not have spending guidelines, you may find yourself outspending your income. By setting up a budget for the year, you know how to allocate your dollars into categories. How will you divide the budget into categories of interest? To have a category for "advertising" in which you lump all advertising costs may be fine for your accountant at tax time, but it might not provide the detailed information you need to make long-term business planning decisions.

Under "advertising," you may want to have subcategories for various kinds of advertising. When you know how much you spend for each type of advertising as well as the sources of your income, you can determine which types of advertising translate into profits and which do not.

As a wise business planner, you will want to determine the return on investment in each category. For each dollar you spend, do you see a return of 1, 2, 10, or 20 commission dollars? That return is referred to as "leverage." The better the return, the better leverage you have achieved. How successful would you be if for every dollar you spent in a given category, you achieved 50 cents in return? Many agents ignore that ratio.

How do you analyze your income and expenses so you can redefine expenditures? It is critical that you categorize all of your expenses and income to have a clear picture of your business model. The more precise you are in identifying the classifications of expenditures, the easier you can see what value that expense brings. You need to identify areas of concern in your budget. Where are you spending money currently, and how can you change your expenditures without diminishing your results?

What questions do you need to ask to know where to make changes? Pick a category and ask someone else to help consider the necessary questions. After a while, it becomes second nature for you to pick apart the categories to identify areas for reconsideration, becoming as efficient as possible in your spending decisions.

Phone calls are a necessity in the field of real estate. Knowing who is making the calls may help to organize the staff. Sometimes unnecessary calls are being made. Other calls may be the key to bringing a transaction to fruition. Make sure that your staff time and use of the phones is appropriate to the responsibilities of each team member. Learning how people work and assisting them to work more efficiently is important to the systematic evolution of a team response.

Cell phone usage has become essential for every agent. That same technology can now provide access to your database, to the Internet, to e-mail inquiries, and to many other sources of information and communication. If you think walkie-talkies are essential for you and your team, then you may need a specific type of phone. As we have mentioned, the cost of technology changes, and so does its portability. My first car phone cost $2,900 and took one-third of the trunk space in my vehicle. It cost $0.40 a minute to use it.

At that time, I was one of the few agents who had a cell phone due to its cost. Now, some phones are free, and with a two-year commitment, you can get unlimited usage. The cell phone can be your source of access to the Internet for your laptop. Phones in the office can be forwarded to the cell phone or home phone for access when the office is closed. Discounts may be available due to your franchise or NAR affiliation.

Who orders supplies for the office? How are supply needs determined? For what items do you pay an exorbitant amount? Where can you get supplies more economically? What sources will give you a discount, saving you 10 to 20 percent on the majority of your office supply orders? Can supplies be delivered for free, so that you don't waste your time or the time of any of your team members?

What forms of print media are being used? Are these the most effective sources for eliciting client response? Are there several different forms? Are packages with discounts for longer-term commitments available from each vendor? Which entities are supplying the best results? Is there a significant difference in the dollar spent to dollar return ratio between the entities?

Who does the technical repairs for the office? Can someone be found who will group repairs into a less expensive, more efficient package? Or is a plan already in place and you're duplicating the cost? Does the broker have someone on staff to handle the technology issues?

What is the cost and what are the results of your Internet efforts? What are the various sites? What is the cost for each site? How many leads come through these sources, and how many of these leads are converted into contracts? This analysis will determine whether to continue or discontinue the use of each site. Sites do differ in their effectiveness. The number of hits or inquiries is not the most critical issue; the most critical issue is how many of those inquiries actually turn into contracts. Some sites are established to produce thousands of leads. Are you prepared to handle this many leads in a way that produces the desired results?

What is the cost of doing business at your current location? Is there a split in the commission payout? Is it a 100 percent program? If so, what are the monthly fees? Is there a cost for your space? Is there a cost for having nonlicensed staff on-site? Are there costs for using machinery on-site? Is there a cost for using the broker's general staff? All of these fees add up. Would it be advantageous to meet with your broker and negotiate better terms for you and your team? Will your broker permit you and your team to have a branch office under that brokerage? Do you want to become a broker and have your own office? Remember that such a venture would entail a second set of business plans and completely different responsibilities. It is important to find out what you are paying so that you can determine if the location fits you and your team.

How much of the machinery do you own yourself? Is it cost-efficient to purchase, or would leasing be better? What machinery is it wise to have control of versus paying a fee to use? How many computers do you need for yourself and your staff? When you buy computers, how do you identify what configuration you need? Can you get discounts through your membership in NAR or through your franchise, or would ordering online give you a price advantage? Is the software being offered with the computer current and appropriate for your needs? How long will the machine be functional before you need something more powerful?

What is the cost for color copies? Do you use an in-house machine or do you send out to have the work done? For example, we went from paying 50 cents a copy side to the broker to paying 11 cents a side by leasing our own printer/copier. Typically, as newer technology is developed, it becomes less expensive. While analyzing each of these items takes time, achieving more effective cost control changed our business planning regarding when we use color in our brochures, etc. To save time, you may want to hire a company to assist you with this analysis.

How much are you spending on education for yourself and your team? We will talk about the need for education, to stay in the business and advance your professionalism, in Chapter nine. Typically you will not have to travel to attend classes required by the state for renewing your license. Travel, food, and housing expenses will more likely be involved in furthering the level of professionalism for you and your team. The amount you need to set aside for these expenses is discretionary: you get to decide. Certainly, some real estate professionals spend massive amounts on education. The appropriate amount of education for you depends on your implementation of what you learn. Coming home and not applying what you just learned makes the investment not worth much. You may also find home study or Internet-based classes that will fulfill at least a portion of your educational needs. A good example is the first two classes in the Commercial and Investment designation (CCIM) requirements. You save time and the cost of travel by taking the courses online, and the course fee is less, too.

Some categories are basic overhead costs. You must control your overhead by finding the most economical way to run your business. You will, however, always have some overhead that does not show a leveraged return. Having someone assist you in finding the most efficient, cost-effective methods of providing your overhead may, in the end, prove to be a wise investment.

The list of categories in the Business Budget Analysis found in the Appendix is not meant to be complete. It is simply a starting place. It has columns for your budgeting and for your spending. The format works well in a computer spreadsheet.

Establish the categories that work for you. You may want more refined information regarding certain aspects of the business than someone else may need. The information flow is for your benefit, so design the categories so that they break down information the most effectively for you. The major categories will be your most frequent reference point. Design your categorizations to give you the information to conduct your business with the greatest insight possible. If you later need to make adjustments, the choice is yours. Not paying attention to your budget and your actual expenditures could be fatal for your business.

Keeping Track of Your Leads

If you have ever missed an appointment because of poor calendaring or control of your leads, you know how frustrating that is. You work hard to get that lead into your schedule, but then something happens to your system, you miss the appointment, and all of your effort is useless.

One missed appointment I will never forget. Somehow the information about a meeting with a prospective client never made it into my electronic scheduler. In fact, I scheduled someone else for the same time. That day, while I was out on another appointment, a very angry woman was sitting in a hotel waiting for me to pick her up. She got in touch with my office but refused to leave a name or number. I could not remember any appointments that I was missing. I still do not remember the woman's name, and I have never found her missing appointment file. I did, upon further thought, remember a phone conversation when I had promised to be available. But that lead is lost. The woman in the hotel will never be my customer, and she has probably never stopped telling the story of the real estate agent who left her hanging. I am sure some unsuspecting agent got quite a wonderful opportunity that day—and a commission check.

How do you make sure that you don't lose your leads? What procedure can you follow so that you will never have the same feelings I had when I heard about the angry prospect waiting for me to pick her up?

The reason I first hired licensed assistants was because of the pink slips. Years ago, all phone messages were kept on pink slips. They piled up high on my desk. I found it impossible to get back to everyone interested in doing business with me. The ones that were pressed to do business immediately got my attention. The ones who needed follow-up got less of my attention. Those who were months away from taking action lay at the bottom of the pile.

I discovered that I was at a point in my career when having licensed assistants to handle inquiries and leads from buyers and sellers made sense. I then ended up with more time to create more leads. Apparently working on the business, not just in the business, brings results.

It is important to keep track of all your leads and how these clients' needs are being handled. Technology provides wonderful features to remind us what we need to do next. We do not have to sit there and wade through pink slips. Instead, we can organize leads and place them on our electronic calendars, which will remind us of all of the tasks we have promised to perform.

This means that we must look at our electronic calendars and organizers regularly. It also means that we have to complete the daily to-do list daily. We have to enter the times when we have committed to do something for a client in our electronic calendar. We must develop the discipline to enter information in the calendar and have the entire team do the same.

It can be easy to identify which team member has responsibility for specific buyers and sellers. That team member's name can be a category in the electronic file. All of the phone numbers, fax numbers, e-mail addresses, physical addresses, names of family members, birthdays, anniversaries, and the source from which this lead was derived can be stored for future retrieval at any time.

If everyone who deals with this file leaves notes, then the file includes a history of all contact with the client. The records are even dated and time stamped should the need arise for verification of these contacts. It becomes a legal record. In today's world, lawsuits are potentially a part of your real estate future. The more complete the notes, the better your protection from any future misunderstandings. Also, the next person working with a client will understand what has gone on before.

All documents, including contracts and all accompanying communication, can be scanned into the file to create a history of the printed and written materials involved with each client. We can know more about and keep better track of every client than ever. However, unless the systems for entering information are defined and followed by all members of the team, the record will be haphazard at best. A procedural list of requirements should be put together, so every staff member has a complete set of instructions on the appropriate method of maintaining records. Accurate, timely record keeping should be part of every team member's job description as well.

Deciding what software or Webware to use is only step one. An outline of how all team members should use the record-keeping system is step two. Reviewing the records to verify compliance is step three.

Once you have this system in place, regularly reviewing with each team member what is happening regarding their contact with clients will not take long. Whether there are 2 or 22 on your team, a regular review of both process and results is very important.

How Will You Know How Many Leads Come from What Sources?

One of those little tedious tasks that is so important is keeping track of why every client chose you and your team. The easiest way to track this information is with a sheet or report that every member of the team turns in on a weekly basis. Someone then needs to compile the list for the team for that week.

It is, like most reports, easily formatted for a computer spreadsheet. Across the top, you can list the various sources of business. Each source needs to be tracked so you can accurately assess what works in your business setting. Use a short team meeting to identify the potential sources of your business. Should new sources of business arise that are not yet on your list, just add them to the form.

Signs are one of the primary buyer sources. The more listings you have, the more sign calls you will receive. In some areas, you can use directional signs to point to your listing. This allows you to add to the number of signs you have up and, therefore, gives an impression of more business. Although buyers call because of signs, sellers also perceive you as being dominant in their area if they see your name often. Riders on signs that say "Sold" tend to draw calls from potential sellers, who see the sold property as a statement of your results. They also want one of those "sold" riders on a sign in front of their home.

Fliers in a box attached to the sign are critical tools to elicit that phone call. The more impressive the flier, the greater the chance of getting a phone call. Print out your listings at other locations on the back of the flier to show potential buyers other properties that may better match their criteria.

Lately, some agents have been using riders that read "Sold By" above the sign with their name. They get permission from the buyer to put the sign in the yard for several weeks after the closing. That way, they get additional advertising at very little cost.

Other Techniques to Gather Sources

Another, growing source for leads is lead-generating Internet sites. This source can have quite a high number of respondents. However, stealth sites may generate a huge number of leads but, after contact with these prospects, far fewer transactions than other sources. The key to turning these leads into buyers and sellers is the speed with which you get back to them and the consistency with which you keep in touch with them. Some of these Internet platforms can automatically respond to people who use the site and even send regular updates to these individuals. Potential clients should be able to remove their name and e-mail address from the database whenever they choose. Potential clients have not necessarily been referred to you by someone who has worked with you before. Don't assume they have an emotional tie that keeps them loyal, and respond quickly and consistently to demonstrate your professionalism.

Number 1 Expert (also known as Best Image Marketing) provides a source of business that exceeds the results of many other sites. The site is well designed, and its placement and terminology place it high in search engines, making it more frequently used than other sites. After spending money on another site for over a year with little to no result, my son decided to try Best Image and received his first lead from the site in less than two weeks.

If you choose to have several different sites, then you need to track each of those sites separately. Only then can you identify which of these sources is returning the greatest profitability.

As we have described previously, print advertising will not give you your highest return of income for the amount spent. Tracking your most effective forms of print advertising will be very helpful as you develop your budget for each year. If a particular publication does not provide sufficient return, then you should discontinue your advertisement there and put your money in a more productive direction.

Postcards are a convenient, less expensive means of making contact with a certain segment of the potential client market. You can send them to past clients, potential clients in a farm area, and current clients. Postcards are a short-view item for the public; typically one member of the family—whoever goes through the mail first—sorts through the mail, giving attention to each piece for three to seven seconds. A postcard may catch a bit more of the individual's attention than a letter in an envelope. Also, instead of being thrown away immediately, it may be saved so that another family member can read it.

Postcard series have worked for some agents. Some series have recipes. A family can keep the postcard and use the recipe for years. Contact information for the agent or team is also on the card, so that as long as the family has the card, they know how to reach the agent.

There are all kinds of topics for these postcard series. Some are simply informational. It may be a notification of daylight savings time. It could be an announcement of a special upcoming holiday. It could have a measurement conversion chart, perhaps showing ounces and cups versus liters. It could be tips for unusual cleaning substances for specific situations.

Another possibility is a postcard with a discount for another cooperating vendor. The postcard could offer a two-for-one dinner coupon or a discount for a hardware store or a free ring cleaning at a local jewelry store. The other vendor is helped by bringing in new clients. You gain by providing something of value to the public and improving the chance that a recipient will hold on to your postcard for more than a few seconds.

One of the series of cards can be of the new listings acquired by the agent or team. The "Just Listed" series is typically sent out to the farm area or the client list. This effort can influence potential sellers, as it shows you are consistently marketing the homes you list. It also can introduce buyers to your inventory as it appears on the market.

You can also send "Just Sold" cards. This continues to show the community your effectiveness. The more of these cards that appear in the mail, the more local buyers and sellers will perceive that you're doing good business. It is important to have an idea of the number of inquiries made based on your postcards. Ask your clients. You can't tell how effective these approaches are unless you actually analyze the response sources.

Keeping Track of Listings

It is of utmost importance that you identify trends and events with your listing inventory. You need to know how your sales statistics compare with those of other products in the MLS. Do your homes sell at the same rate, faster, or slower than the rest of the inventory? Do your homes sell for less than, the same as, or greater than the MLS percentage of list price to sale price? Each of these statistical comparisons gives you detailed information on how you are doing with your pricing and marketing in comparison to other agents in your area.

This information may also provide you with data to differentiate yourself from other agents. Suppose that you sell your listings on average ten days sooner than the average for the MLS—the public needs to know that. Suppose your sales price is significantly higher in comparison to list price—the public needs to know that, too. Suppose that you are not ahead of the MLS or even behind it. If so, then you need to know why. With this information, you can change your marketing strategies to improve your results.

Keeping Track of Buyer Sales

You should also know the relevant statistics for the buyers you represent. You should understand what percentage of the contracts you write for buyers are unsuccessful and why they did not work. In some cases, the buyers may make offers that do not reflect the market. Sometimes their offer reflects their ignorance or uncertainty about a new region. Other times, their response is reflective of their perceived "needs," not the true value of the property in question. It is imperative that both the agent and the buyer realize what the offer represents in the mind of the buyer. Often, the structure of the offer holds subliminal reasoning that the buyers themselves don't understand, and understanding their emotions is the basis for educating the buyer.

Is the market skewed towards buyers or sellers? Each market has its own concerns. In each, the agent needs to explain the market conditions to the buyer to encourage a reasonable offer. If you are proactive about educating buyers, more of your clients' offers will be accepted. Some agents insist that their job is to procure the desired home at the least cost for buyer. In some market environments, that philosophy may turn out to be frustrating for the buyer when their offers are consistently trumped by better ones. Analyzing the number of buyer offers presented versus the number accepted can lead the agent to some significant insights into successful or unsuccessful methods of preparing the buyer.

Compare these statistics over a three- to five-year period. When these are tallied on a month-by-month basis over time, trends emerge that may give insights into your business flow. Note the months when offers are made as well as the months that closings occur. Each set of statistics adds insight for the design and development of the business.

Keeping Track of the Market

One of the most valuable assets an agent can have is the ability to interpret the market. Looking at the market and wondering what's happening and what's going to happen is just not useful.

Some insight into market trends can be found by reading the statistics in the MLS as often as every day. A small number of listings coming on the market and selling quickly creates a seller's market. A large number of listings coming on the market and selling slowly signals an oversupply or a buyer's market. One common way to judge the market is to ascertain how many homes have sold in the last month, identify how many homes are currently listed in that same category and area, and then divide the number of homes under contract into the number of homes that are actively available. The result tells you the number of months of inventory that are on the market. For example, if an average of 5 homes were sold last month in the area similar to the home that you are looking at, and 15 such homes are on the market, then divide 15 by 5, and you have a 3-month supply. If 60 homes are on the market and 5 sold last month, you have a 12-month supply. As the number of available homes changes and the average number of homes that go under contract each month changes, you can forecast the trend of the market. Don't remain oblivious to market trends. Far too many agents are unfamiliar with them until after they are well underway and show up in the local or national media.

Real estate markets generally transition in five- to seven-year cycles. Becoming familiar with how these transitions generally develop and the phases that most often follow will give you a historical perspective on the market. Having experienced a very tight, seller-oriented market, we now hear shouts of calamity because the next phase is occurring. That phase is a slowdown in sales and a settling of prices due to more homes being in inventory. This is a normal phase in the real estate cycle, and agents who have been in the business for a long time have experienced several such phases.

Eventually, the next phase of equalization will occur, bringing the number of listings and the number of buyers into a more even balance and providing for a shorter marketing time frame and prices that are stable or rising slightly. This completion of the real estate cycle provides continuity to the market. The panic over predicted calamity changes to calm and confidence in real estate values.

Staying up to date about these changes is important. If you do not understand where you currently are in the real estate cycle, anticipating upcoming changes is difficult. And there will be changes: that is the constant.

Watching national and international news, keeping abreast of changes in the financial picture, and staying informed of the popular perception of current issues is another significant responsibility of the alert agent. It is not always the interest rate that is important; it is the perception of that rate that matters. In the early 1980s, interest rates jumped to 18 percent. I was able to procure a 12.5 percent rate and was thrilled. Today, I would feel cheated to pay such a high rate for a residential mortgage.

Although the rates were very high, we still sold homes. We earned a living and assisted those who wanted to sell and buy homes to achieve their goals. It is the attitude, not the altitude, that makes the difference. It is how people perceive the rates, not how high the rates actually are, that makes the difference. During President Reagan's term, rates dropped into single digits. During most of my lifetime, rates hovered just below or just above the 9 to 10 percent range. Today's buyers become jittery at the thought of rates climbing to the 7 percent level. History shows that this would affect their buying power but would not eliminate the opportunity to purchase.

By understanding the current market and interpreting it on an historical level, the agent becomes an instructor for both buyer and seller. This instruction requires insights into the history of real estate as well as accurate knowledge of the current situation. As the market makes its normal shifts through the cycle, the agent's responsibility is to anticipate changes, modify business plans, and educate the consumer to the realities of the market.

When the Market Changes, What Do You Do?

There is never a given formula for market changes. They work through at their own pace, and you must adjust your marketing to match the market. When the market is overloaded with too many listings and not enough buyers, some agents become tortoises. The agent pulls in on all marketing and tries to stay away from spending any money on advertising. Allan Domb, an agent in Philadelphia, decided to do just the opposite. He increased his advertising, finding special pricing from vendors because other agents were diminishing their ad sizes. He found that his methods increased his market share. Even though there were fewer transactions, he got a higher percentage of them.

Each change in the market requires some adjustment in your marketing plan. Adjustment and revision are always a part of the business for any agent. It is important that as these adjustments are made, each change is constantly monitored and re-evaluated to understand its effectiveness.

Change for change's sake is not the aim. The aim is to promote the agent's presence in the community and knowledge of the current real estate market. As the public becomes confident in the agent's professionalism, the number of opportunities to represent a buyer or seller increases dramatically.

Your Marketing Plan

It is the obligation of the agent to market their availability and skill. If agents do not do a sufficient job of selling themselves to the public, then the agent will have very few opportunities to market homes.

Every agent has different ideas about the best ways to market himself to the public. My philosophy is that you have to put your name in front of enough people, often enough, and creatively enough, to show potential clients who you are, what you do, and how to get in touch with you. The better you complete this task, the more real estate you can market and the more buyers will seek your assistance.

There are several philosophies about how to present yourself to the public. One, espoused by Mike Ferry and those who follow his example, is cold calling. In effect, you are trying to find those people who are currently prepared to use real estate services. Another philosophy is that of farming. Just as it sounds, farming is the process of planting seeds within a given geographic area with the anticipation of harvesting those leads as the people in that area grow to accept your presence. Still others feel that target marketing is the way to go. This means that you identify an element of the market with which you want to work and proceed to contact the individuals within this market parameter. One concept encouraged by several national trainers is to work by referral only. This means that your marketing is actually to people who already know you, including those who have already used your expertise, so that a cheerleading squad acts as a finders' group for your future transactions.

Each philosophy has its merits. Each requires certain disciplines to provide success. Unfortunately, the most dominantly used marketing technique is to let the broker do the marketing. This approach generates limited return that is further divided among others who take the same approach. This is why the 80/20 rule, used by the largest number of agents, works so well.

Cold Calling

Cold calling is contacting individuals who do not know you and securing their allegiance if they should have a real estate need. Cold calling can be done by telephone or by going door to door. Cold calling is exactly that; these people are not hot leads. You do not know up front if these people have a current real estate need or will give you the name of someone else they know with a real estate need.

Cold calling takes discipline and a tough skin. I know that my own response to telemarketers is not pleasant. Doors may be shut in your face or phones may suddenly go very quiet. Discipline makes this program work. Practicing scripts that elicit positive responses is very important. You must become skilled at helping people become interested in communicating with you very quickly. It is imperative that if you choose this methodology, you are committed to working it for a specific amount of time each day. This type of prospecting must be done consistently. If 1 out of every 100 people has a real estate need, then you will probably talk with 99 who will not have that need. Cold calling requires an internal mechanism that is confident that people are not rejecting you. They are merely saying that they have no need for your services. However, your presentation while speaking with them will help to determine if they will search for you when they do have a need or search for someone else.

Not many individuals are sufficiently committed to cold calling to make it their primary means of acquiring business. Those who make the commitment are successful, because they find people who respond positively to the call or the knock at the door. Making a consistent effort to contact people who need and want your services is critical. A daily routine of three to five hours of cold calling does pay dividends. Mike Ferry suggests that if you are going to make phone calls, that you do it from a standing position. He feels that your voice reflects a more businesslike tone when you are standing rather than sitting. Those who follow his advice create desks at standing height, where they can write notes and have other materials right at their level while standing.

I have several friends who follow this methodology and are very successful. The overhead for this type of endeavor is lower than for marketing through printed advertisements. Cold calling does require long-term involvement; it is a career commitment. The search is never ending. Timing makes the difference; therefore, cold calling must be worked regularly. The discipline of consistency is difficult for many. Should you choose to follow this style of marketing, it will be imperative for you to make cold calling a daily routine to achieve success.

Farming

Farming is the process of contacting homeowners in a specific geographical area multiple times in a variety of ways.

The consistency of contact makes the homeowner aware of the name and phone number of the agent who is marketing to this area. When you make your name easily remembered or retrieved, then potential clients are more likely to call you to handle their real estate needs.

Making creative contact with people so that they initiate a call is a completely different marketing method than cold calling. It requires a solid understanding of the marketing process to raise awareness of your name to the "top of mind" efficiently and effectively. In top-of-mind marketing, you create a direct link for individuals, so that any thought of real estate needs brings your name to the forefront.

Some agents are unsuccessful at farming, usually because they do not make enough contact in the farm area and allow too much time between contacts. Successful farming requires consistent contact through a variety of methods over a significant period of time. The shorter the time between contacts and the more often contacts are achieved, the more likely homeowners will call you for their real estate needs.

We have previously discussed the concept of shelf life in the material that is sent out. The longer a person looks at the material, the greater its impact. The more people in a household who view the item, the more likely some member of the household will call you or refer you to a friend, even though they never have met you or used your services.

Some agents find that giving a regular update of market statistics for that geographic area or subdivision causes more family members to take a look at their communication. In many cases, individuals will hold on to this material for future reference. It may be put into a file or possibly even hung up with a refrigerator magnet.

Speaking of magnets, the magnet has some of the best shelf life of any item that can be distributed. Yours should feature some reason for an individual or family to keep it on the refrigerator alongside all the other magnets. Just having a business card format with your picture and information will probably not keep you hanging around. We use an over-sized annual calendar that is also a write-on board. Family members can leave messages to each other on the refrigerator or write down phone numbers. We also include a slot for our long, thin message pads. Many people use these for their grocery lists. A magnetic pen also comes with the set so that it can be handily attached to the refrigerator. Under the message pad is an invitation for the homeowner to call us if they need more pads. The refrigerator magnet will be seen by all members of the family several times every day for a year. Sometimes we find that people keep calendars from several different years on their refrigerator because of the write-on feature.

Another great type of magnet shows the days that school will be in session, off for vacation, or shortened for any reason. Parents love these. The name of the school and principal should be on the magnet along with the office number, the nurse's office, and the absentee line, if there is one. In most cases, schools will agree to send this home with the students within the first week of school. This saves on delivery cost for the magnets. You will need to get district approval and then approval from the local schools involved. Each school will have a different magnet with their own information on it.

With a name like Baker, I have tried to keep things in the kitchen. We have delivered cutting boards, measuring spoons, measuring cups, and all other kinds of kitchenware. Giving an item that will be kept because it is useful extends its shelf life.

Determining which geographic areas will be your target zones takes some thought and preparation. You need to know the number of homes in each area. You need to decide how large a farm you can handle. It does no good to have a huge farm but contact them only rarely or sporadically. My wife and I ended up with a group of farm areas totaling 6,500 homes, but we started with a subdivision with 425 homes.

You should do an analysis of the homes in your intended area. Check the MLS to see how many homes transition in a year. Of all the homes that sell in the area, does an agent or several agents seem to have the area already well in hand? If so, then you must decide if you have the stamina and the desire to penetrate that market to take market share away from them.

You may want to select several different areas because of the price parameters in each. If you select only one price point to market to, then you may find that sometimes that price point is less active. By having a variety of price point areas, you spread your efforts among several potential market trends. If the less expensive homes are most active in the marketplace, then you want to be participating in that market. If median-priced homes are becoming active, then you would want to have some of those. The upper range may generally be the slowest category, but it will still reward you well for your effort.

Another reason for having a variety of price ranges in your marketing plan is that sellers also tend to be buyers. And buyers in many cases have homes to sell. When you cover a variety of price ranges, you work with the "move up" and the "move down" buyers. You establish a wider reputation than by just working with a particular price point. Lower-priced sellers may have the impression that you do not want to work with their price range if you do not let it be known that "large or small, you sell them all." You want those who intend to buy higher-priced products or who want to sell a higher-priced product to know that you are, in fact, an expert in that area.

Howard Brinton, another national sales trainer for real estate agents, is very much into the marketing styles of those who farm. He provides a monthly tape featuring an agent he has recently interviewed. Each agent tells the story of their business plan and why they have selected that business format. Often these people have a history of farming.

Farming requires an input of capital. It costs money to make all of those contacts. It takes time for all of the marketing to penetrate the mindset of those in the farm. You will not receive maximum results with the first item or letter you send out. Instead, results take time. Results will come sooner, however, if initial contacts are made more frequently. I know of a study that determined which agent appeared to be dominant in the minds of homeowners in a particular area. When the results were completed, the company doing the study sent a postcard every week for eight weeks to this same group of people. These postcards featured a nonexistent agent. Then a follow-up study was done. At the end of the eight weeks, the nonexistent agent was found to be the most dominant in these people's minds.

Farm marketing takes time, but it works. It takes money to get started, but the return can be very large. It is one of several methods of gaining the opportunity to represent buyers and sellers, and many top agents around the country have had success with it. You may want to consider incorporating it into your business plan.

What Is Target Marketing?

Target marketing is the process of selecting a group of people with whom you want to do business. Once you identify the parameters of these people, meaning the qualities that all group members have in common, then you need to determine how to reach those particular individuals.

For example, some agents want to work primarily with doctors. That classification is easy to identify; just look through the phone book. You may want to see if you can join an organization to which this group of people also belong. You may want to find out if this group has an existing newsletter, newspaper, or Web site. Is there a way for you to be in that publication or on that Web site? Certainly, there are opportunities for you to purchase ads. Is there also a way that you could do a feature article on the nature of real estate investments in the area? Is the publication in need of sponsors?

When I moved to Tucson, I became very aware of the area's large Hispanic population. I found that high-quality representation was not readily available for this portion of the community. Out of the 90 agents who were then in the office I joined, no one spoke Spanish. It became a goal and a part of our business plan to involve the Hispanic community in our sphere of influence. Very quickly, we hired a young man who had been born in Colombia, spent two years on a mission for his church in Chile, and spent most of his years after age 11 in the United States. We set about to make certain that the Hispanic community understood that we were available to service their real estate needs and could do it in Spanish or English.

Through some investigation, we found that there was an Hispanic Chamber of Commerce. We went there and met with the executive officer. We found that their newsletter to the 600 businesspeople who belonged did not have a sponsor and what it would cost to sponsor it. Now, we have an article in the newsletter every month.

We found that this organization wanted to set up scholarships for young people in the community. Their goal was to give out 20 scholarships each year with each scholarship worth $1,000. They counted on members and the business community to provide funds for these scholarships. We offered to provide a scholarship every year. They were delighted with the offer, and we now attend the annual luncheon and are recognized as students are awarded their scholarships.

Our team also has a moving van that clients can use on local moves at no cost. On the truck, we display our special telephone number for Spanish speakers. Every print ad contains this message, and our Internet sites also display that information. As a result, an ever-increasing number of Hispanic buyers and sellers are using our services.

In addition, we have found that title companies and lenders are excited to be involved with us. We now have a list of those lenders and title companies who have bilingual representatives that will work with us. We are, therefore, creating an ever-increasing source of professional services available for our clients in this target market.

Spanish-speaking individuals are not the only non-English-speaking market that can be targeted. Every burgeoning town and city has groups of people with a common heritage who would like to find those who understand their traditions and their language. Ron Garber, whom I have mentioned, had several bilingual and multilingual members of his team. This gave them a wonderful edge in providing personalized service for Chinese, Japanese, Indonesian, Vietnamese, and others who wanted to work with professionals who understood their lifestyle, culture, and language. Over the years, I have discovered that people of certain Asian cultures have very specific beliefs about homes. An agent aware of these cultural beliefs, which include the direction the door opens and the history of the home, can make finding and retaining these clients so much easier.

Second home buyers are a target market for some agents. If you are in a location where many people want to own a vacation home or second home, then a positive move on your part might be to target this segment of the population in your business plan design. Florida, the Carolinas, the Gulf Coast region, ski resorts, hunting areas, golf centers, and lakefront and boating areas may all be locations that draw second home buyers.

You need to know where people come from to buy homes in your area. The local chamber of commerce may be an appropriate source for this information. You might want to ask agents from those areas to coadvertise for buyers in your area. Giving them a referral fee for locating buyers may be an inexpensive way to generate a constant flow of business.

It would not take much time for you to set up all of the agents from a specific geographic area in your system to receive e-mails on a regular basis. You never know whom they may meet who would like to do business in your area. When your area is mentioned, you want to be the agent they remember and recommend.

Once you are in touch with buyers from these areas, you may be able to set up your MLS to update them about any property that comes on the market and fits their parameters. This automated feature saves you time and money. You will be constantly reminding them that you exist. They will think that you are checking out all of these properties, when in reality an automated system is doing the work. A little time and money keeps these potential clients on your list.

These people will not only buy—at some point they may also sell their properties that they use as second homes. For example, they may want to upsize or downsize their properties. Staying in touch with them while they are at their primary location is important. You can usually get a list of out-of-state property owners from the title companies. By placing these people on your list of contacts and keeping them in touch with the local market, you will find that many will come back to you for your services. These individuals may also have friends and family who will decide to purchase or sell in your area.

You may want to focus on the retirement community. The baby boomers are changing locations, homes, and hobbies. You may find that you can assist them in the process of downsizing their habitat for their new phase of life. They may be looking for a second home or an entirely new environment. One couple who are friends of mine have just downsized; they just need a place to come back to locally when not on the road with their motor home. They had a home to sell and needed a smaller home in a secured community, because they will be gone months at a time.

Your target market could be investors. You may want to be in touch with agents who specialize in this area. Individuals from their contact lists may want to branch out to your marketplace. You want both clients and agents to understand the benefits of investing in your community. Perhaps you see great expansion or appreciation ahead or that individuals can easily generate positive cash flow from properties in your area. In my region, a projected 67,000 new homes will be built over the next seven years. Land is a valuable asset in that area. We have a small number of acre lots that currently have manufactured homes on them. They sit in the middle of an area that will soon be absorbed by one of the local cities, and commercial property surrounds them. Though they are not zoned commercial, they no doubt will be. The properties are being sold at what some local bankers consider a high price. Within a block, however, acre lots with commercial zoning are going for two to three times the price. Some investors would take the risk—and thank you for it.

There will always be families that have had some financial disaster and are threatened with foreclosure or some other immediate need to sell, which would redeem them from their current problem. Finding these people and connecting them with investors who are willing to take over their homes can be a service to them. It is important not to set yourself up to take advantage of their disaster. Still, your services are needed, and you can target this audience as a part of your marketing plan.

One friend of mine is in touch with attorneys. She handles homes for divorcing couples and for estates. Her primary source of business is the referrals she receives from this specific group of attorneys. They feel confident that she is fair and professional with their clients, and as a result, she has a constant flow of leads. Because these leads are directed by a professional in whom these families have already shown confidence, she can feel confident they will choose her to transact their real estate business.

Jean Shine is an agent who has designed her business around the military families who flow in and out of her community as they receive their assignments. She has made it a practice to find out what she can do for soldiers and their families in her community and those stationed around the world. She has sponsored Christmas trees that are decorated and sent to military personnel serving far from home. She's encouraged elementary school children to write letters to those stationed abroad. She has collected old phones, helping to turn them into cash for calling cards for people in uniform serving away from their families.

Jean has targeted military families as her primary business source. She has not only benefited greatly from transactions with these individuals, but she has also contributed to their lives. Her target market is not just a business decision; she believes in her clients and what they do. She is a professional to the utmost degree.

Targeting this market takes some involvement and knowledge of the military lifestyle as well as the benefits afforded veterans in financing their homes. If you have a major military facility near you that you feel you can service, then you may want to get in touch with agents who service this target market in other areas. Other agents can be a major source of referrals, if you understand the system and interact regularly with those who also have made it their mission as well as their target market.

Some individuals like to zero in on the first-time homebuyer. It is quite the educational opportunity. Most first-timers have never studied the process of purchasing homes and have little knowledge of how financing works. Therefore, if this is your target market, it is imperative that you understand the full process and are prepared to convey this knowledge patiently to potential home buyers.

Top-of-Mind Marketing

Top-of-mind marketing establishes yours as the one name that comes to mind when the subject of real estate is raised. It results from seeing your signs, reading articles about you, and hearing positive stories from friends and associates about your expertise.

Achieving top-of-mind marketing should be the goal of agents who want to establish themselves as the dominant agent in the area. What do you feel others know about you and your real estate career? What do you *want* them to know about you and your real estate career? Few agents seek to minimize their impact. It is important to decide what you will do to provide maximum public exposure for your name and your expertise.

Unfortunately, many agents are shy or have been taught that saying positive things about themselves is impolite or offensive. Your competitors will not play fanfares on the trumpet as you walk by; they will toot their own horns. Your obligation is to let the community know how good you are at selling real estate. They need to know that you are a professional with great experience and ability.

The newer you are in the field, the fewer bragging rights you may feel you have. So brag about the impact your company has had. Make sure that the public is aware that you are working with outstanding agents. Include the combined statistics of the office. Although a solely boastful campaign is not what the public is looking for, they also don't want to work with the most inexperienced agent in the field. They need to feel confident in your skills and talents. Creating that sense of confidence is your responsibility. Some will come through your advertising. Some will come through working with prospects and demonstrating your skills.

You may not aim to be top of mind to the entire community. Are you top of mind to your target audience? How does this group of people perceive you? Those with whom you want to work need to know you as the dominant expert in the field. They want to consider you their realtor for life. They want to know that at any time they could contact you and have any real estate question answered honestly and professionally.

Perception Is Reality

It is not always reality but perception that is important. Soren Kierkegaard, an existentialist philosopher of the 1800s, indicated that it is not the relationship between two people that is important; rather the perception of the relationship by each party that matters. Whatever the relationship is in actuality is affected by the perception of each individual regarding the actual situation.

In real estate, we deal with the same concept. Who is actually the top agent is not as relevant as people's perception of you. The public's perception makes all the difference in terms of their desire to be involved with you. Once that perception is created in the public's mindset, it becomes a powerful force driving business either toward you or away.

Your use of media, signage, and your public involvement is critical in setting the public's perception. You may want to do a survey before you begin any new marketing campaigns to find out what the public in your target marketplace already thinks about you. You may need to hire a company to do the survey so that the questions will elicit a true response, not one biased due to your involvement or your staff's involvement.

Once you have a feel for the public's perception of you, you need to decide what you want them to believe about you—what perceptions need to be changed? One friend of mine in Dayton, Ohio, found that the public perceived him as being far too busy to handle their individual needs. Subsequently, he used more casual attire in his ads. The formal look of his suit and tie and the professional settings in previous ads had conveyed an unapproachable image. Casual attire and nonbusiness settings with his family brought about an entirely different perception. He had not changed, but his image had changed. As a result, his business increased.

What you think they think may not be what they really think at all. Understanding more clearly the public's view of you, and what you want that view to be, clarifies your approach to marketing. Image making needs to be a part of your business plan. If you have no idea what the perception of you is, you can do little effectively to change it.

When Do You Use Print Ads? Internet? TV? Radio?

Choosing the type of advertising you will use and budget for is a critical part of your business plan. Print ads are the form of advertising most commonly used by real estate agents. Generally, the cost is based on a per-page format for each publication. Many magazines are designed to market real estate. These magazines are generally placed in public settings for easy access by potential clients.

The *Real Estate Book* is a small version in this format generally printed in full color. It tends to be one of the more expensive of the magazines on a per-page basis. *Harmon Homes* is a nationally published magazine that is generally printed in black and white. As such, it is one of the least expensive of the magazines. In many areas, price lures many agents to advertise. They satisfy many of their sellers with the number of times their listing is in print ad format.

We have found that *Homes and Land* is one of the more effective magazines. Because we keep track of results from each of these print formats, it is easy to decide which ad dollars have the highest leveraged return. Should you choose any of these or any of the multitude of local magazines, you must analyze which form of print advertising in which locations brings you the greatest number of calls and what percentage of those calls translate into closings and, therefore, income. An additional point of interest is the amount of income generated for the amount spent in each magazine. Different formats emphasize different products (land; manufactured homes; lower-priced, midrange, and high-priced single-family homes, townhouses, or condos).

Specific homes may require different magazines. Advertising waterfront properties in boating, sporting, fishing, or surfing magazines may be advantageous. Horse property may be advertised in magazines geared towards equestrians. Homes located in skiing communities may be profitably advertised in skiing magazines. Golf course and country club properties could be advertised in golf magazines. Homes in communities geared to active adults (generally at least one owner must be over 55) could be advertised in retirement magazines. If the home is located in a community that features its own airstrip (some of which have taxi strips to the home and a private hangar), then magazines oriented to the private plane owner would be appropriate. Ads in specialty magazines tend to be more expensive, so leveraging a good return is unlikely on a lower-priced property. However, if you are target marketing a specialty type of property, then you may find that placing a print ad in a specialty publication gives you more credibility among members of the target group.

Newspaper ads are becoming less and less effective. Unless the newspaper has its own Internet site that publishes the print ad to enhance its visibility and viability, then placing an ad in the paper can be very expensive. Larger, localized daily newspapers are generally quite expensive, sometimes costing thousands of dollars per page per printing.

When I was in Illinois (Naperville, a western suburb of Chicago), I advertised in the Chicago *Tribune* every Friday. In those days, newspaper advertising was a much more effective way of getting calls from interested buyers and sellers than it is today. I advertised in a regional publication of the paper that was geared towards DuPage County, where I was located. I was the only individual agent who placed a full-page ad once a week. In those days, the cost was a thousand dollars a week for a full page, and that was a discounted rate because I signed a contract to advertise 50 times a year.

Because I had to draw the public's attention to the ad, I used what is referred to as the "Tupper Briggs style" of advertising. Tupper Briggs is an agent in Evergreen, Colorado. He began using ads that did not involve any of his inventory but instead used catchy phrases with pictures of Tupper. In many situations, we simply duplicated Tupper's ads. Finally, we began to create our own. One picture was of me in a classroom. There were no other people in the room. The caption read "In a class by himself." Another was of me in a cornfield with a caption of "Outstanding in his field." Another featured me standing with my arms out to either side. The caption was "Anatomy of a professional real estate agent." Alongside the picture were other designations: "Two arms that reach out to assist buyers and sellers, two eyes that see problems in a contract before they arise, two ears that listen to every buyer's or seller's concerns . . ." That ad was designed by my daughter. One ad had me sitting at my desk with my hair disheveled, my tie down (I wore ties in those days), my desk piled with papers, and the phone to my ear. The caption was, "It is 9:00 P.M. Do you know where your realtor is?" This style of advertising got the public's attention. People would call to set up an appointment and tell me that they would look each week to see my creative ad. I did this for 15 years. The return was wonderful, until we hit a slowdown in the market. When the slowdown hit, we were also getting an upsurge in Internet advertising. Finally, we switched out of newspaper advertising to a more efficient and effective use of our dollars on the Internet.

Some smaller local papers, some of which are weekly papers, are much less expensive to use and, therefore, do not require the same sort of leverage to be effective. The key is to watch the return. If you do not keep track of your sources for calls and your sources for closings, you have no way to track the results of your advertising investment.

Some homes receive special attention by being advertised in unique places. The *Wall Street Journal,* for example, can attract notice for very high-end homes. You must be sure which homes qualify for this type of capital outlay. If your target market is high-end homes in your area, then you may have more of a reason to use this type of marketing than most agents.

The Internet is now the advertising site to which any astute agent should pay the most attention. The use of home computers, high-speed Internet access, and the increased savvy of the general public has pushed the real estate businessperson into Internet marketing in a huge way. Individuals now can get to the inventory in almost any town in the United States with little difficulty. Soon, a buyer will be able to bookmark their favorite site and search for homes in any town in any state and in most countries around the world.

The ability to show a home's assets through extensive photos and even conduct a moving tour of the interior and exterior of the home gives potential buyers an enormous amount of information prior to entering the home. Buyers can even select a home without ever having walked through the front door.

In addition to the photographic benefits of the Internet, with the advent of the the computer among MLSs, potential buyers can narrow their search to those homes that fit their specific criteria. Parameters for their search can include the price range, number of bedrooms, number of bathrooms, size of the lot, subdivision, schools, number of garage stalls, whether it has air-conditioning or not, whether it has a conventional pool or spa, whether it has community facilities, whether or not there is a fireplace, whether the yard is fenced, whether or not horses are allowed, or just about anything that might be important to them.

When I started in the business, it was impossible to search for all of these parameters and come out with a realistic list of homes available. Now the public has access to so much information, that the process of locating a suitable home requires much less time from the agent.

As technology improves, agents must increase their ability to understand and use the Internet. Many people want to sell you their sites. Unless someone is continuously improving your site, it will become outdated very rapidly. The public wants ease of use, access to pictures and information, and rapid responses when they e-mail you with questions. With today's technology, you can know when an individual enters your site and when they e-mail you within seconds. Your speed of response may very well be the deciding factor as to whether the prospect does business with you. If you wait until the end of the day, or worse, the next day to respond, then you may lose that client to another agent who is equipped to respond more rapidly.

The Internet will be the main way that buyers and sellers reach you. Your Web presence, your placement on search engines, the technology you have chosen to provide access to your information, and the ease of use of your Internet presence determines if prospects mark your site as a favorite and return whenever they have a real estate question.

Unless you are going into a full-scale marketing campaign with radio and television, you may want to limit your investment in these areas. Those who have taken out contracts with television stations are committing themselves to significant costs. In these areas, consistency is important. An agent in our area has made a large commitment to television. She has been successful in catapulting her business to a very high level. Because we are not privy to other agents' budgets and profit and loss statements, we cannot ascertain the profitability of this venture. Her commitment level would seem to put her television advertising budget well over a $100,000 a year. She may find that the leverage is working for her. Should you decide to enter this area of advertising, make sure that you are well financed for the long term.

I tried radio advertising in Chicago. The radio station was advertising its availability to create ads while I was driving my car one day. I found the concept intriguing. I called and committed for three months. I loved hearing myself on the radio. I would perk up each time I heard the ads. But I spent $6,000 for the ads and did not get a single phone call from them. Radio advertising turned out to be an expensive ego trip. Again, be sure to track your advertising responses. Analyzing the numbers is the only way to determine whether the return is worth the investment.

Can You Work "By Referral Only"?

It is difficult to work only on the basis of referrals when you begin in the real estate business. You have no one who already knows your capability in the field. You may have come from another industry where you have a lot of contacts that you can count on for referrals, but this approach generally gets you off to a slow start.

Once you have been in the business for a time, you can begin to work with your past buyers and sellers, your vendors, and other agents to generate leads. Warm leads are more fun to work than cold calls. Referrals start with a level of trust, because someone else has introduced you.

Those who advocate this method of doing business do not encourage you to go out and create a large advertising campaign. Instead, the focus is very small, on those who are your friends, your cheerleaders, and your advocates. These are the people who want you to succeed and will assist you in any way they can. When you have a large enough group of these people and you stay in contact with them, you will find that they will be your bird dogs for business. They will go out of their way to give someone in their circle of friends an opportunity to use your services.

Socializing with these people, sending thank-you gifts to their offices, and keeping in touch with birthday, anniversary, and seasonal cards makes a big impression. Your job is to keep your name in front of these people. Even your most ardent supporters can fall away if they feel forgotten. Your strength is your consistency of contact. Having them on automatic mailers, on automatic e-mail communication, your newsletter list, and your party list will pay handsome dividends both in friendship and professional loyalty.

Marketing to Past Clients

There are many ways to market to those with whom you have already done business. Obviously, these people should be in your database systems. You need to know everything about them that you can. How many children do they have? What are the birthdays of each member of the family? When is their wedding anniversary, if they are married? When is the anniversary of their moving into their home? What are their pets' names? What are their favorite activities?

You may want to invite them to a client party. It may be just for adults, or it can be for adults and children. You can provide them with tickets to sporting events. You may find a movie that you want them to see. You can bring together small groups of individuals who you think have something in common. Maybe they come from the same state. Maybe they have the same occupations. Maybe they have the same number of children. All of these things could be a reason to bring them together to get to know each other and, in the process, share stories of your professionalism during their business with you.

When I got into this business, I did not remember that I had past customers. I made no effort to recontact these people, and I became a part of the 80 percent of the agent population that does not stay in touch with former clients. As such, my level of repeat and referral business was relatively small. Once I opened up the connections and made the effort to contact these people, however, amazing things happened. They began to do more business with me, and they began to invite friends and family to do business with me. The exponential growth far exceeded my expectations.

One of our most popular innovations was to provide a condo for our clients to use in Scottsdale while we lived in Chicago. It was marvelous to have them call and schedule a week at the condo. It was a three-bedroom, two-bath condo with a two-car garage. The complex had its own pool and exercise facility. You can imagine what happened at work for these people when someone asked them where they were going on vacation and their response was "to my real estate agent's condo in Arizona." That certainly got a great deal of attention and provided inroads for future business.

Fostering business from past clients and from their friends and family members is a primary source of income for the professional real estate agent. It develops a deep sense of loyalty in the potential new clients. It is a basis on which a real estate business can grow and flourish.

How Much Education Do I Need?

The amount of education an agent needs depends on how much the agent is willing to learn from those who are already in the field. The basic education required by most states provides definitions of terms and information on the laws that govern the agent, and it allows the agent to be licensed. The knowledge from these classes will keep the agent out of difficulty if the agent adheres to the lessons. However, these classes do not provide information on forming a business, how to build a list of potential buyers and sellers, and how to build a team.

Continuing Education Is Required

States require a specific number of hours in continuing education, typically some number of hours in the fields of contract law, fair housing (making sure that selling practices are nondiscriminatory), ethics, disclosure, etc. These classes are absolutely essential in keeping the agent up to date in areas of concern.

In disclosure classes, agents are taught what items need to be shown as areas of concern, disclosed to potential buyers, and brought to the attention of buyers if observed. Disclosure forms are typically provided by the state or by local associations of REALTORS®. In some cases, individual brokers will have additional disclosures for buyers and sellers. When given to potential clients, explained, filled out, and signed, these forms become a way for the client to acknowledge that this disclosure has been made.

In some areas of the country, radon gas is quite an issue. The government has certain criteria for acceptable levels of radon gas on EPA studies. Homes typically can be modified to bring these levels to an acceptable number, but sellers and buyers may find that the expense must be considered in the contract.

In some areas, swimming pool installation carries with it a series of local, county, or state requirements for safety. It is important that each buyer and seller understands that these rules exist and agrees to abide by them.

Pest levels, such as termite infestation, must be understood by the parties involved. Some areas have few pests, while in other areas, such infestations are almost inevitable. The potential for destruction of the home due to infestation needs to be known.

Airport proximity is another area of concern. Noise levels can be overwhelming if the runway patterns are close to the home. Once the disclosure has been made to the buyer, it is up to the buyer to decide the importance of this issue.

Fair housing is a very important area of concern. These classes need to be repeated over the years. Nuances in the laws change. It is important for every agent to understand and practice fair housing ethical conduct. No potential buyer or renter should have to experience prejudicial conduct on the part of a real estate professional or any client of a real estate professional.

Ethical conduct on the part of agents includes their level of service to a client. Every area of concern needs to be covered. Agency laws differ from state to state, and they have changed over the past decade due to concerns about the representation of buyers. Whatever the service provided, that level of service needs to be explained and understood by the client. The explanation must be in writing and signed by the client.

A real estate agent must have a great deal of knowledge to provide the best possible service to the client. For example, knowing the tax consequences of real estate transactions is extremely important. Most agents are not accountants or tax specialists, and they need to make their limitations clear to the client. However, agents can give a basic understanding of the direction transactions need to go to provide the best possible result for the client. For investors, an agent's knowledge of 1031 exchanges could be important. The tax consequences of an owner's selling a primary residence needs to be understood by the agent and conveyed to the client. Always after any explanation, the agent must mention that they are not an accountant or tax specialist and the client is responsible to consult with their own tax expert. Tax laws change, so an updated level of understanding is essential.

The quality of an agent's education is important. These are not just state requirements that need to be fulfilled. These are areas of basic information that are essential for you to understand. Taking the minimum hours required to renew your license is only the beginning. You should become an expert in every area of concern.

How Do You Decide Which Designation to Pursue?

What is a designation? Designations indicate that you have taken the required classes to achieve a certification granted by a particular authority. The National Association of REALTORS® has a variety of designations that give increased knowledge in a variety of areas through the required classes. Designations are not required to do business as a real estate agent. They do, however, provide an increased level of knowledge and an indication by an industry authority that you have achieved the level of knowledge to be granted the designation.

The National Association of REALTORS® provides education classes that have been approved for these programs. In these cases, organizations are approved by NAR to provide the training and authorize the granting of these designations.

The CRB is the Certified Real Estate Broker designation. It requires a series of classes that enhance the broker's understanding of his responsibilities and gives additional training on running an office or company.

The GRI designation is Graduate of The REALTORS'® Institute. State associations generally sponsor the classes required to achieve this designation, which requires a considerable number of hours in class on a variety of topics designed to provide extensive training in marketing and organizational skills. The topics can cover tax law, financing, new construction, reading blue prints, and more. This comprehensive set of classes enhances the agent's general knowledge of the practice of real estate sales.

CRS, Certified Residential Specialist, is a designation dealing with residential properties and the knowledge required to establish a thriving business in the field. It is a tight-knit organization in which those who have the designation look for others with the same designation in other areas of the country for referrals. In addition to classes, an annual conference is offered. The curriculum and class offerings are revised periodically to update those with the designation.

The CCIM designation, Certified Commercial Investment Member, is for those who want a better understanding of the implications and requirements of commercial and investment undertakings. The classes are extremely intense and provide the designee with NAR's equivalent of a master's degree in the area of commercial and investment real estate. An agent typically needs two to five years to earn this designation. The agent must also meet a serious level of production over time to obtain the designation.

e-PRO is a designation with a technical orientation for the use of the computer and the Internet. It enhances the agent's ability to market services through technology. As noted previously, the use of the Internet in the sale and purchase of real estate is increasing at a phenomenal rate. Not having the skills to use technology in the marketing of properties and servicing clients' needs is a disadvantage in a highly competitive industry.

ABR, Authorized Buyer's Representative, is a designation that has come about from a new understanding of the agent's responsibility to the buyer. In years past, the agent had a fiduciary responsibility to the seller even if working with the buyer. This concept was referred to as subagency, and it was part of the laws in almost every state. The agent was responsible for informing the seller of anything revealed by the buyer to the agent. Buyers did not understand this relationship, so a level of mistrust developed. Buyer advocacy groups worked to change these laws. Now the practice in nearly every state is to have agents who work with buyers be able to represent those buyers. They are, therefore, not required to tell everything that is provided by the buyer to the seller; in fact, the contrary is now the case. The classes for this designation go into great detail on the required levels of loyalty and service that the agent needs to provide the buyer. Agents may choose to have buyers sign an agreement much as sellers sign a listing agreement. This gives the agent a guaranteed level of loyalty for the period of time and parameters covered in the agreement. This change in agency has been one of the most important changes in real estate law in the past two decades.

The NAR supports other designations as well. Selection of the coursework that will best suit you is an individual matter. It is important that you continue to advance your professionalism throughout your career in real estate. Ongoing education gives you the knowledge necessary to provide the best service for your clients and instills in them a feeling of security, because they know that you are consistently updating your skills and knowledge. A surgeon who does not take classes and gain information on new medical techniques is not a doctor that I want operating on me. I want the most up-to-date data to be available for that medical professional, just as your clients want the agent helping them with valuable transactions to possess the most current knowledge and skills in their profession.

Other organizations offer designations. The Employee Relocation Council, for example, has the designation of CRP, Certified Relocation Professional, a program that trains experts in the relocation policies that employers, lenders, and third-party relocation companies use. Some independent organizations also create and sponsor courses leading to their own designations. Before venturing into these classes and committing to the annual dues, be sure they are what you want. I suggest that you contact those who have already attended the classes and gained the designations to see if they feel the experience was beneficial.

Designations are not the final word in education for agents, but they do provide a level of professional training that raises an agent's level of expertise. Though the public may not comprehend the meaning of the alphabet soup after an agent's name, clients will recognize that the agent with these designations has considered continuing education important.

Mentors

Mentors are individuals who have knowledge from which we can gain. These people have experience that helps us make wise decisions in our business planning and execution. Many such individuals are available to give you guidance. The key is to find someone with whom you feel comfortable and confident. This person is the one to whom you will look for ideas and encouragement. Perhaps you'll choose more than one mentor. Unless they have similar values and ideas, you may find yourself torn between seemingly contradictory philosophies.

I have found that there is not just one method that works. Many approaches are successful. Most mentors select one method and emphasize that method only. Unfortunately, some agents try to mix and match concepts that are not necessarily compatible. You want clarity in your vision of how you will implement your business design. You do not have to attend every seminar from every mentor who comes your way. Knowing this will save you money and time. If your approaches do not mesh well, then you are not optimizing your dollars or maximizing your time.

Most mentors will ask you to step outside your comfort level. You will do things you haven't done before. You may not like to do some of the things they suggest. However, without moving beyond your current comfort level, you will find yourself on a plateau where you don't achieve further growth.

Brian Buffini, Howard Brinton, Mike Ferry, Pat Zaby, David Knox, Dave Beason, and Tom Ferry are some of the most prominent mentors in the field of real estate. All of them have successful ideas and plans. You can typically hire a top agent who follows your chosen mentor to coach you, so you have one-on-one help from a proven professional. I have personally chosen to follow Howard Brinton and his Star Power network. He does not take a rigid stand but instead invites you to look at many styles in place with outstanding agents across the United States and Canada. You choose which techniques to implement. Pat Zaby uses Microsoft software in his presentations on how to maximize technology for today's market. Dave Beason is well known for his series of hundreds of letters that you can download and edit to make them personal. David Knox has created a number of videos to assist in educating your clients. You can lend them to a client and educate them without even being in the room. Tom Ferry has created quite a following with his emphasis on business design. He is one of the trainers with a premier coaching structure to assist you. Mike Ferry follows a consistent structured methodology involving cold calling that many of my friends follow and find very successful. Brian Buffini has a program of intense effort to jump-start you on a 30-day road to success.

Each one of these mentors—and there are more—takes a different approach, yet their adherents find success in their efforts. Mentors provide large-group seminars and conferences to introduce their concepts. They also have videos, CDs, and DVDs you can purchase for private listening and viewing. It may take a while for you to determine which of these mentors will be your guide, but the effort in choosing will set the tone for your business career.

Personal Coaching

Personal coaching has been increasing in real estate for the last ten years or more. It takes many forms. Personal coaching most often occurs on a one-on-one basis but can be also done in small-group sessions. The reason you choose to have a personal coach determines the style and content of your sessions.

Many real estate agents want to be responsible to check in with someone regularly regarding their fulfillment of their business goals. When you know you have to report on how well you achieved your desired or assigned tasks to reach your goal, your motivation to complete the task increases dramatically. These individuals are held to the completion of a series of goals to which they have committed from the previous session. Mike Ferry and Tom Ferry each have coaching setups in this style.

The coaches who work with Star Power and Howard Brinton will work with you on the basis of your expressed needs. You may want to have business coaching in the form of business planning. You may also want coaching that fits a broader spectrum. These coaches are referred to as "life coaches," because the spectrum of discussion can be very wide. These are not meant to be therapy sessions but are opportunities to have someone with an outside perspective look at your world. Sessions may involve more of a questioning of your situation and viewpoint than a series of answers. Sometimes the questions elicit insights regarding your life and provide you with potential responses for situations of concern.

Dr. Fred Grosse was my coach for eight years. I was introduced to him by Bob Wolff, a friend and agent in California. Bob organized a group of us to meet with Dr. Grosse six times a year for two days each time. Dr. Grosse introduced all kinds of concepts for enhancing not just business professionalism and control but also control of our lives in every area. His insightful messages caused many of us to stop working at a frantic pace and start to enjoy the fruits of our labor. Rather than seeing our businesses slow down, we found that life became far more interesting and enjoyable when we let our real estate businesses fund our life dreams and goals. I watched while agents modified their business plans, taking more time off. They took trips that they had not envisioned possible. They became more profitable as they engaged in what Dr. Grosse referred to as "Dollar Productive Activities." He taught us that if we used the concept of focus, our increased production during work time provided increased personal time. He taught us that if we were to rate our life activities on a one-to-ten scale, then we could increase our daily activities into the ten range simply by calendaring them into our days. The results of my eight years of learning from this life coach rearranged my conceptualization of life and redesigned both my business plan and my life plan.

Recently, I have asked another coach to work with me. Her name is Debbie Yost. She has been a real estate agent for years. She and her husband were also in a coaching group with Dr. Grosse. I know we share a vision for life. I need, however, to have someone else assist me in seeing things I am not seeing. That is the job of a coach. Debbie has decided to do coaching full-time and has become certified in that field. I have watched as she has assisted agents by physically visiting their offices, observing how they function, spending time with their staffs, and analyzing their business plans. I have found her insights to be absolutely enlightening. Her interviews with my staff and the ensuing suggestions for me to work better with them have been extremely valuable. I've felt another infusion of excitement for the business and for life since using her services.

Others like Debbie have found excitement in assisting those of us who want to stay in the real estate business. Their insights can have resounding implications and serve as a jump-start on the next part of your career.

Hiring a good coach is not inexpensive. The cost can be anywhere from a few hundred dollars a month to several thousand. The value of this investment is difficult to perceive, until you are in the midst of the experience. The resulting focus, attention to business, and freedom for personal growth and development are priceless. You may want to speak with someone who has a coach and see how they are responding to that individual. Your goals for the coaching experience will help to determine whose style best fits your needs.

Reviewing
Your Results

Setting up a business plan is wonderful. It is the basis for developing a successful asset of which you can be proud. Implementing the business plan is the next step. Great ideas are only dreams unless implemented in an orderly way. Finally, analyzing the results of implementation is a tedious but necessary task to fine-tune great ideas into amazing ideas that reap great rewards.

Reviewing the results is a constant, never-ending opportunity for the businessperson. You need to review your results at least weekly to see if any modifications should be made. A complete review of results is required each month. You need to know how many leads came in and where they came from. You need to know how many leads transitioned from prospects into clients. You need to know how many transactions were written and accepted that month and how many actual closings took place. You need to know the expenses and the income for the month.

Monthly Reviews

The items named above are the critical issues that need to be accounted for on a consistent basis. Forms to have you track this statistical information are provided in the Appendixes. Ultimately, the information will be input on forms that can be used over periods of months and years to analyze the consistency of the business and trends that seem to recur. Once you have established the habit of generating a full report each month, the process will become as natural as getting out of bed in the morning.

Staff members should be able to have this information in hand at the click of a few computer keys. Once you have established the forms, very little input is needed. In fact, a software program like Microsoft Excel can generate reports automatically from a single input. The review takes less and less time as you become accustomed to the process. If results are meeting expectations, then smiles are the only necessary response. If results are exceeding expectations, grins can be added to the response mechanism. If results are not meeting expectations, then further analysis rather than frowns are the appropriate response.

It certainly is possible that a month does not seem to fit the pattern of the plan. If a second month shows the same results, then you must consider adjusting the plan.

Quarterly Reviews

Even though you may see a change from one month to the next, you may want to wait until the results are in from a third month to see if the change is a fluke or a trend. If the change is a trend, then you must decide what to do to prevent any negative direction from permanently damaging your year. What you do and how much of a modification you make depends on the degree of negative change. Some business analysts insist that any change should be made on a trimester basis, so you have a four-month basis for determining the direction of the change.

If the change appears to be consistent, then you must decide an appropriate response can end, modify, or reverse the change. Obviously if you are observing a positive change, then you must decide if any action can magnify it. By knowing the direction of your business and how it compares with other, similar time frames, you can maintain control of profits and losses.

Each modification needs to be measured by specific information. If you do not keep track of your sources of leads and your ultimate sources of business, you cannot track your investment of dollars and their returns. You must know how much you are spending per source and each source's net return. Without this information, you are looking at variations without the ability to pinpoint the issues that need to be dealt with. The specific details will help you to refine your business plan and create the highest leverage possible for your investment of time and money.

For example, if your emphasis is on farming but you are not getting the desired results, then you must analyze your process. Do you not contact your farm area often enough? Are other agents more efficient than you in the farm area? Do you need to put in more effort or withdraw and try elsewhere? Those decisions can only be made if you have detailed information with which to analyze your results. How much are you spending on farming? What is the return from your efforts? Is the return $3 for every $1 spent, or $10 for every $1 spent? The analysis of the number of transactions and the amount of return per amount spent combine to give you basic parameters for your decisions.

Each aspect of the business should be able to be broken down in fine detail. The more detail that can be analyzed, the closer you are to making the wisest decisions for your business. Quarterly analysis gives you a better control method than waiting until the end of the year.

Annual Evaluations

An annual, full-scale evaluation of your business is an absolute must. It is important for you to identify your goals for the year. It is also important to restate your budget for the ensuing year. Having a general number to be spent is insufficient. You need to know what you are going to do for marketing. You need to know what staff you will have: Are you going to stay at the same staff size, grow, or trim your staff? You need to know what your office overhead will be. You need to know equipment expenses for the new year. Will it be important to purchase your own color copier? If so, how will that affect your marketing, and will it cost you more or less than you are currently paying?

These decisions will be based on the past year's results and also a comparison with prior years. Every year added to the comparison gives you trends in the market that you need to analyze to project your future investment in the business. A step-by-step, item-by-item analysis give you a complete understanding of your business. It provides you with insights that you cannot achieve in any other way. A general look at the business does not enable the precision in decision making that business owners need to be successful. Knowing how the business is functioning is a requirement for the agent who is building an asset that is a viable, salable entity.

Using last year's business plan as your basic outline, sit with your financial counselors or business partners and make plans that will enhance your wealth in the business. These plans may include the tax ramifications for purchasing equipment or building your own office building. You may want to decide what to pay before the end of the year to limit your taxable income for the current tax year. Certain vehicle purchases can be written off more quickly than others. It is important to have someone who can lead you in the decision-making process. Why should you pay for something in December instead of January? Are the laws changing and when, and will the change help or hurt you?

Do you have business partners? Do you need cross-insurance in case one of you dies or is incapacitated? Should you hire a consultant who can assist you in this field? How do you value the business if you have a business partner? Do you have a buy-out plan in place if one of you wants to leave the business but the other one does not?

Are you currently a corporation, sole proprietorship, LLC, or partnership? Why would you function under one system versus another? When is it time to change the nature of the entity due to liability factors or tax ramifications? Do you have a line of credit for further growth or to cover unexpected changes in the market? Having your own board of advisors is important. Bankers, attorneys, accountants, and investment analysts all could be a part of your internal planning team.

In reality, as a businessperson and not just a real estate agent, you need to make many decisions. As an employee, you would not need to make these decisions. Many agents structure their lives as if they were still employees. Your asset is significant. In the future, you might choose to sell the business or bring in someone as a partner. You will need to have the business fine-tuned, humming along, to gain the interest of someone else. If you don't understand your business, how do you expect someone else to understand it or get excited about it?

Long-Term Planning

Having a history of your business is important as is having a plan for the future. When you have a road map and a destination in mind, it is easier to get where you planned to go. There may be some detours along the path, but you can make adjustments and return to the predetermined route in time.

Where do you want to be three years from now? Five years from now? You should begin to develop the vision of where you would like to arrive. This preplanning process places you in the driver's seat instead of just being a passenger on the journey. Adjustments in the plan are natural and fully acceptable. Not planning is unacceptable.

How do you want to fund your retirement? What will be required to meet these needs? With less than 5 percent of the population able to live at the level they would like in retirement, retirement planning should be a priority.

Are you envisioning a large team with you as the CEO? Or are you envisioning yourself with a partner who will take the dominant position in the business while you lean back and take a more relaxed posture? Will you be working in earnest to expand the business? Your view of the future is absolutely critical. As stated before, you may change your perspective and decide to work towards a different goal as you move along the path. You will, however, need a path to move along to avoid aimless wandering.

11

Your Exit Strategy

The process of leaving the business may be far in the future for you. I know that I have promised my wife that I will not show another home after I reach the age of 101.

Realistically, somewhere along the way, I will decide that we should travel and enjoy more time doing nothing work related. Currently, a five-year plan for me contains visions of developing several teams in various locations. I love the idea of being a CEO or co-CEO.

I had looked ahead for myself and knew when I relocated to Arizona that I would get back into the real estate business. It was quite a shock when, just as I was heading into this venture, I found out that I had cancer. I planned on beating the disease, but I knew that while I was fighting, I needed to have someone working with me who would have the same zest for the business that I have. I wanted someone I could train and someone who would have the stamina to carry out the business if I were incapacitated.

My daughter introduced me to the husband of one of my son-in-law's co-workers. They were at a Christmas party, and while they were talking, my daughter found out that this young man, though still in college, was considering a career in real estate. We made an appointment to meet, and I was impressed with his work ethic and his desire to succeed. I invited him to be my partner.

My plans were based on a desire to re-establish a real estate business. I had been in real estate sales for over 20 years and had made a great living. Once we had decided to work together, I had an opportunity to teach him the business. He would still be finishing college for a year and a half. He had never had a real estate license. The business and its nuances would be new to him. You might wonder why I would choose someone like this to be my partner.

I have a history of taking people out of college or fresh from other life experiences and bringing them into the real estate business. I had done it half a dozen times previously. My son-in-law had worked for me for a number of years. Although the experience was good for both of us, his business plan had always been to get into banking. I felt that his intentions should not be changed by my desires, and so when we left Illinois and went to Arizona, he and my daughter moved with us. It was then that he changed his career.

I find that the fresh ideas and energy of young people invigorate my concepts of the business. The ideas I come home with from the many educational classes I attend require an ability to adjust my vision and have those around me adjust theirs. These young people have that capacity in rich abundance.

Starting all over again gave me a chance to restructure my entire point of view for the business. In those days, such a move was considered unusual. Today, the concept has caught on. I see a friend in Vail, Colorado, move to Naples, Florida. I watch an agent on the East Coast build a second team in the San Francisco Bay area. I watched one good friend move from Connecticut to the Carolinas and begin a stunning career in a resort area. One friend decided that she wanted to move to the town where her new husband lived instead of having a commuter marriage. She only moved three hours away, but it was a new market. She was able to sell her business and establish herself in her new location, providing the social setting she wanted as a newlywed. What was once unthinkable is now prevalent, because agents are thinking about their future in intervals longer than a week. All things are possible. They simply take imagination and commitment.

Your only limitation is what you decide it is. You can change markets. You can change the types of real estate you sell. You may move from residential to commercial. Sitting down and taking a look at where you are and where you want to be is one of the great opportunities of life in this part of the world.

How Long Do You Want to Work?

Ultimately, you will be leaving real estate sales. For those of us committed to working until we are 101, it could be the day that we take our last breath. For those with that desire, enjoy the experience. It is a choice you can make. This is an enterprise from which you cannot be barred as long as you are ethical in your business dealings, pay your dues, take your continuing education classes, and make the effort to find buyers and sellers.

For others, other enterprises will become more desirable than selling real estate. The process of making that decision will take place over years of business planning. Nonetheless, it needs to be prepared for.

Will you hire a partner who will run the business while you are paid residuals for having built it? Will you outright sell the business to a current competitor? Will you bring in someone new to the area and have them purchase your business?

Again, your decision is just that: your decision. Part of your decision making needs to take place over the years, so that you can prepare your business for the transition.

What Will Your Business Be Worth When You Exit?

With all of the effort that you have put into your business, if you should decide to exit, how will you do it? Will you simply walk in one day and say to your broker, "Here are the keys to the office. I am finished. I am retired"? That is an easy way out of the business. It frees you to do whatever you want. You have no ties. You have no obligations.

Wouldn't it be nice to have a business that was worth some money? When you have finished developing that business and have worked in that community for a long time, will you leave behind a group of people who still want to do business with you or your colleagues? Will others in the real estate business give you money to let them take over the business?

Insurance agents sell their book of business. Accountants and attorneys sell their practices. Why can't you also sell your real estate practice and gain from the asset you have developed? In the past, there was no pattern of agents selling their businesses to other agents. In the mid- to late-1990s, the practice began on a very limited basis. Prior to that time, agents did not view themselves as business owners. Brokers were the business owners. Finally, however, agents began to view their businesses as owned by themselves rather than by the broker. Agents began to assume that the business they had built had value.

Determining how much a business is worth suddenly became a concern. Currently, no banks will provide loans for someone to purchase an agent's business. They will give lines of credit against real collateral, but they do not have a history of analyzing the value of an agent's business. If it were a real estate office, then the broker's business would be evaluated and potentially funded by a lending institution. It is amazing that there is such a difference between the sale of the office versus that of an agent. Lending institutions are simply inexperienced at funding this kind of transaction.

As new opportunities are introduced for agents to purchase other agents' businesses, parameters will become better defined, and banks and other lending institutions will begin to engage in this endeavor.

Determing the Value of a Business

Some business brokers valuate businesses for other business owners. However, finding people with the experience to look at the dynamics of the real estate agent's business and come up with a defined value is difficult.

The value of a real estate agent's business is defined by a simple formula: Take the average net income over the past three years and multiply it by a value factor of zero to four. The value factor has a number of components. This number defines the base price we work with to value the business.

Your business may not be showing an upwardly moving profit, yet someone might like to take over the business. There may be no defined price placed on the business if zero is used as the value factor. Still there can be a value for both buyer and seller based on the amount of business engendered when the business changes ownership. The payment of value might more simply be done through referral fees after a comarketing plan has been put into place between the buying and selling agent. The referral fee can vary and so can the number of years for which it is being paid. Many issues define where in that formula of valuation your business is found.

Is the business in your name? Does everyone who calls expect to speak with you and do business with you? If so, then your business is actually worth less than if the public simply expects to be taken care of by a member of your team. If the business is based on you, your presence, and your personality, the next owner will have trouble replacing you.

Is your net a high or low percentage of the gross income? The higher the net percent of the gross, the better the value of the business. The net for two businesses on an average over the previous three years may be $250,000 dollars each. If one has a gross income of $1,000,000 and the other has a gross income of $500,000, then the one grossing $500,000 is more valuable. The reason is that the buyer will not have to expend as much to net the same amount. The amount of risk required to achieve the same results is less for the business demanding the smaller gross income. Although this is important, it is not the only concern.

How do you generate your business? Are the calls coming in to you, or do you have to make cold calls to gain clients? If the new buyer will have to cold call on a regular business to obtain business, then why does the buyer need to purchase the asset to get the business started? They can make cold calls and achieve similar results without the investment of purchasing your business. However, if the team leader is not making the calls but team members are, then the substitution of team leaders can take place transparently, increasing the business' value. The system is already in place to achieve results, whether the team leader is present on a given day or not, create value.

The higher the number of transactions achieved by helping past clients or having past clients refer others to you, the higher the value of the business. Repeat and referral business indicates that the business is intact and functioning regularly. It does not depend only on new leads to generate business. Part of this process depends on how often you are in contact with past clients. A business that is regularly in touch with its client database will undoubtedly have consistent, recurring business, and its value will be higher. A database that is used to being contacted and is used to being encouraged to produce referrals is of greater value than an identical database that an agent does not contact regularly.

When I did not pay attention to my past clients, my return business from them and their referrals was about 16 percent of my annual transactions. When I decided to stay in touch with these people and invited them to return to see me at a client appreciation party, the number went up to about 48 percent. Because this source is traditionally the least expensive method of generating business, its profitability is higher, and the value of that enterprise increases.

The more consistent your staff is, the greater the value of the business. If you are retraining staff every few months, then the incoming owner will not have the history and professionalism requisite to carry out the highest level of service to future clients. A long history of team loyalty speaks well for their attitude. Such loyalty will pay dividends for the new owner just as it had for the previous owner. The team's enthusiasm for the goals and achievements of the group will spill over into the minds and hearts of their clients.

How well have you taken care of your database? Is it intact? Do you e-mail or mail these people on a regular basis? The gentleman from whom we bought our business in Tucson is a great salesperson. He has a great mind and can remember nearly everyone with whom he has ever done business. The problem is that he never was interested in learning how to use the computer. His past clients, we were told, were placed in the database by members of his staff. He did not regularly contact this group, and we found that many names and addresses had never been input or updated. In addition, the backup disks upon which we were relying were unusable. We had to spend many nights in a garage going through files, pulling out the previous five years of information from closing folders. We were amazed at the knowledge he had of these people after long periods of no contact. We continued asking him questions about them, and he filled us in on what he could remember.

Once we had hand copied all of the information from those five years of files, we input the data into new software. Next, we mailed correspondence to this group of past clients. We mailed first-class so that we would get new forwarding addresses or be informed if no forwarding address was available. Some clients were still at the same locations; others weren't. Some lost clients were never located, while others were found through Internet searches and local phone books.

When your database is being contacted regularly, it is much easier to detect changes in the information. Much of the value of an agent's business is in the accuracy of the database and the loyalty that past clients feel for the team. The confidence level, achieved by outstanding service and communication, must be continued on a regular basis. These individuals need to be clients for life.

The business we initially purchased in Tucson was worth a good deal, but it would have been worth more had the proper steps been taken to have a clean, up-to-date database. Maximizing the value of your business can be readily accomplished with advance business planning. You can have the systems in place to make the difference between a value of $100,000 to $200,000 versus a value of $400,000 to $500,000. Those additional dollars can go a long way to make your retirement dreams a reality. A new owner will gladly pay the difference for a business that is set up to be self-perpetuating. A business that transitions easily from one owner to another is definitely worth the increased investment.

When systems can be easily duplicated, the operation is referred to as being "like McDonald's." It can be reproduced, and it will function the same for the next person in charge.

What Else Do You Want to Do with Your Life?

Real estate will not be your only interest in life. We have spoken before of the "big rocks" that each of us has. What is your next big passion? What do you want to do that will bring peace to your soul and provide meaning to your existence?

Once you begin to define these things, you will begin to see a scene open for you, and you will be prepared to move to the next act of this life play. I have friends who have taken new adventures into their daily routine and have found a renewed zest for life.

There may be a time when you simply tire of the daily routine of the business. It may suddenly become less challenging. You may discover a need to experience a different phase of life. You may have a need to relax on a beach. You may find a need to add variety and intrigue. Maybe you want to skydive or climb Mount Everest.

You may find it difficult to leave the addictive adrenaline rush of the completed transaction. You may never see yourself totally removed from the scene of real estate but may desire to play a different part in the process. Do you want to train someone new in the business? Would you like to provide someone with the expertise at a very young age to receive recognition as one of the "30 Under 30," exposed to the real estate public through the National Association of REALTORS'® magazine articles? Maybe your daily routine will change, but the charge you receive from participating in the ongoing business will remain strong.

You may find a burning desire to pursue another field of endeavor. Do you want to go on and get your doctorate in another field? Would you like to be a life coach and influence the decisions of interesting and talented individuals who shape our society like my coach, Debbie Yost?

Whatever position you desire, only a few of us will want to sell real estate until we take our last breath. Although real estate sales is a part of our lives, it is not our lives. Looking to the future and seeing the wonderful opportunities there is important for each of us.

Deciding as far in advance as possible what your next part of life will look like and what it requires will help you prepare to exit from the business. You may still want to dabble in the business for a while without having the primary role in running the organization. Or you may want to be totally released from any involvement. The choice is yours.

The Exit Strategy Questionnaire

Whether you will have a partner and residual income, sell to another agent and use the sale's proceeds, or walk away and leave your business without any continuation is your choice. No one else can decide for you. In case you should decide to have someone else continue your business, I have designed a series of questions that I believe will help you achieve your goal.

Each year in your annual planning, you should go through these questions and see if changes need to be made to optimize your preparation for that eventual transition.

Question 1: How will you know when it is time to leave the real estate business?

If you are planning on working until you die, then the answer is simple: When you are dead, you are done. If you plan to transition into another phase of life before then, however, you need to decide what criteria will cause you to make the change. Will it be the amount of money that you have accumulated to sustain you? Will it be a level of boredom with the business? Are certain time frames important in your life plan, such as, for example, a decision that you will retire at age 50? That would be an easy parameter to identify when you have reached it.

The fortunate part of being in real estate sales is that the decision to leave is entirely yours. Unlike many professions that design the time frame of your release—teaching, for example—you have no pre-established end date. Many corporations are forcing early retirement on their employees: prepared or not, here you go. In real estate sales, no one will force that decision on you.

Deciding the time frame or circumstances of your transition is something you can plan, design, and enforce. The earlier you set the parameters in place, the better you can prepare.

Question 2: What part does an annual business plan play in the preparation of your business for transition?

The annual business plan is the opportunity to design the systems and the performance level necessary to achieve the desired value for the business. An annual analysis of your systems and their performance gives you the opportunity to modify them to meet your specifications.

What net have you set for yourself to achieve? Are you achieving that net, and if not, what modifications are necessary to improve the numbers? Can you see where your dollars could best be invested? Are there alternative methods that you can use to improve your net? What new marketing could enhance the bottom line? As you analyze each source of business, which are the most lucrative?

An annual review of the numbers and a planning session for the next year's business plan draws the road map for your success. Once the road map is in place, quarterly reviews are necessary to ensure that you are heading in the right direction.

The business plan should be based on an understanding of your potential exit strategies. Once you are aware of these strategies, you can refine your systems in preparation. The closer the exit time frame comes, the more defined your strategy needs to be. By following a planned strategy, you will have all of the information in place to provide a new partner or a buyer with all of the history, statistics, and general information necessary to give them a clear picture of your valuable asset.

Question 3: At what point do you start preparing for your exit?

You need to begin preparing for the exit the day you open the business or as soon as you become aware that you need an exit strategy. Many agents get into the field without the concept of an exit strategy, other than that someday they will walk away from the business. If that is your exit strategy, then really very little preparation is needed; on any given day, you can just leave.

If you want to accomplish a planned exit and derive financial benefit from the process, however, then it is important to get that plan in mind as soon as possible. You need to begin thinking about the business you want to have in hand upon transition. The question again is: Do you want a partnership, which will bring you continuous income; or do you want to reap a set amount, whether or not your successor continues to be as successful or, possibly, more successful than you have been?

You may want to take the time to shadow others who are preparing for an exit opportunity. You may want to visit someone who has taken on a partner. See which method feels more comfortable to you.

Should you decide to take on a partner, you may want the opportunity to work with that individual for a while before you make a commitment. You may want to test the waters of the relationship, because this will be a long-term opportunity. Once you have evaluated the relationship and the type of person you have chosen to work with, you may decide that this individual either has or does not have the capacity to make your business what you want it to be. No one can make you give your business over to someone who will not carry it on in a fashion you like. Does something about this business partner make you uncomfortable? Do you sense a lack of integrity? An absence of business acumen? A poor personality fit? This is your time to judge this person as your partner for life in the business.

If you decide to sell, then you want to have an extremely high level of confidence in that person. If you are uncomfortable with that individual's replacing you, you will be able to do little about it once you are under contract and they have taken over your business. Once some time has elapsed, it would be difficult for you to come back and revive the effort you had given to the business to bring it back to life.

Question 4: What systems need to be in place to have a smooth transition?

Systems are the process of identifying every step in the activity or activities involved in an aspect of the job. Definitions and guidelines must be in place for every task. When every task is defined and all of the parts of the task are listed in order and explained, so anyone could come in and perform the task, then systems are in place.

Every time you identify another task or series of tasks, the process becomes more duplicatable. Anyone can come in and make things flow at the same rate and with the same precision as those who set up the systems.

When these systems are in place, the value of the business increases, because the following questions are answered and the new individual can easily take over. How do you pay the bills? Who pays the bills? What software do you use to keep track of the bills and print the checks? What reports can the software generate to assist in analyzing the business? Can a profit and loss statement be printed? Can a comparison of budget to expenditures by category be printed? How are the files kept? Are they scanned or are they in paper copy? Can money taken in by source be compared to the money spent on that source? Each financial process that can be systematized results in a better understanding of the profitability of the business. By comparing these numbers on a year-by-year basis, you—and your successor—can understand the consistency of the business or how it is changing.

What happens when a listing is taken? What is the process? Who knows what paperwork the broker and the state require? How do you determine if you have all of the documentation? Who makes certain all of the paperwork is complete and filed? Who inputs the listing? Who takes the pictures? Is the information automatically loaded into Web sites? Do any Web sites need to have the material input by hand? How many pictures do you need for the listing? Are video pictures taken of the home? Who puts up the sign? Who puts on the keysafe? How are appointments made to show the home?

Who contacts the owners to maintain communication with them? How often does that communication take place, and how does it take place: by phone, e-mail, postal service, or personal meetings? What software holds all of the information so that there will always be a record. Is there a system for contacting the agents regarding their showings, and how will those agents respond? Can agents' responses be sent to the homeowners, so they are aware of what potential buyers are thinking regarding the home?

How do you let the homeowner know what is being done on their behalf to market the home? How often will that take place? Do you send copies of ads if the home is advertised? Are there open houses and how many per listing? How are all of the original listing documents kept? Is there a way of making sure that the homeowner has a copy of every document involved in the listing process? Do you plan any kind of activity that allows home sellers to come together and enjoy an opportunity to relax with you?

When you or a team member is working with a buyer, do you follow a procedure to make sure they have all of the information that they need to do business with you in your state? Who keeps track of the required documents? Is there a procedure for keeping track of contracts that are written on behalf of a buyer but that are not accepted or completed for some reason? Who processes an accepted offer? Is an attorney involved or must an escrow company be contacted? Who stays in touch with the lender if one is involved? How do the significant dates in the contract remain in view of the participants? Who brings these dates to the attention of the parties involved? Is there a procedure to make sure all of the dates and time lines are not missed? Who orders the inspections? Who sets up the closing? Who attends the closing?

When a new contact is made by a team member, is there a way to identify this individual and which team member will handle the contact? Can every team member refer to a database to know who is handling which client? Who follows up? Is there a method for reporting this individual to the team leader, and is there a follow-up procedure to review all of the leads and what is happening with them?

How is the team's history kept? Are the statistics on forms that make sense? Who initiates the information? Is it kept in a manner so that years can be compared to each other and history can be understood on a long-term basis? Can information be input just once and automatically distributed to other forms, so that no one has to spend time double inputting information?

Question 5: What assets are available for a successor?

Assets include your equipment. Do you have your own computers? Copy machines and printers? Are they black and white or color? How new are they, and how fast are they? Do you have your own fax machine, or do you use the broker's machine?

What supplies will remain with the team? Do you have paper, envelopes, etc.? In what quantities? Will they be available in the name of the team as it will continue, or will reprinting be necessary?

What listings will remain with the team? How salable are they in today's market? What database will the team have? How complete is it, and how often is it being contacted?

Who is in place on the team? Will they continue with the transfer of ownership? What will motivate the team to continue with the new owner? How long has the team been in place? Are the team members well trained?

Are any vehicles transferring with the ownership? Is any real estate transferring? Are contracts in place for advertising? For leased machinery?

All of these assets will be transferred with the business. The greater the asset value, the more justified is a higher price.

Question 6: What must be in place to show the value of the business?

The easiest thing to compile is a list of all of the physical equipment, furniture, and supplies. There must be an up-to-date list of every item expected to transfer. Some items may seem minor, but they need to be listed to avoid any question by either party as to what has been committed to stay with the team for the transaction.

A complete set of financials for the previous three years and a current year's profit and loss statement to date must be provided. These items should also be summarized on a form so that it is easy to compare the gross and net income for the team for each of the previous three years and determine the business' financial direction over that time frame.

The statistics need to be supported by forms that show the number of listings and the number of contracts written for each month for the previous three years. A set of forms must show the number of transactions closed each month over the same three-year period. This form must also show the number of transactions closed from each source of business during this period. This information shows the shift, if any, in the source patterns. With all of this information, you have an understanding of the business' history, its development, and its direction.

We once purchased a business for which there was a spike year based on the market. When the following year and the previous year were analyzed, however, they were really more meaningful. The average net income, which was disproportionately inflated by the spike year, needed to be adjusted to reflect a more normal market. This type of analysis can only be done in detail when all of the information is available. The seller of the business should know in advance what these statistics show.

In the case of another business we purchased, a large amount of income was attributed to real estate property management. Once the business was purchased, a disproportionate amount of time had to be spent to maintain it, and the profitability of that portion of the business was not commensurate with the amount of time required. We determined that we had to divest ourselves of this aspect of the business so that we could concentrate on the more profitable real estate sales portion. We compiled the information regarding the property management section of the business and contacted a family-owned group who specialized in property management to see if they were interested in acquiring it. They made us an offer we could not refuse, and we could then spend our time in the business that was most productive for us. After selling that portion of the business and recouping some of our purchase price, we could generate sufficient income to increase the business' value if we chose to sell it.

Knowing the business in great detail helps both the selling agent and the buying agent. It is unbelievable, but most agents do not have any idea regarding what they do in business until they meet with an accountant to do taxes. Even then, unless they have a professional relationship with this individual, they may simply be getting their taxes done. It is imperative to know how best to use that year's tax laws and where you exactly stand. We have a regular analysis with an accountant to see where we stand financially and what we can do to enhance the business as an asset and reduce our taxes. Meeting with this individual helps to determine the type of entity you should be working under. Should it be a corporation? If so, should it be a C or an S? Should it be an LLC? Is it best structured as a sole proprietorship? You may change your mind over time. Tax laws change, and so does the state of your business.

It may be important for you to discuss with your financial advisor what portion of your deductible items relate to your personal business planning. You may have the business buy vehicles that you use in the business, but the next owner may not do that. You may have retirement programs that the next owner will not use. These items show as expenses, so they must be identified as items that may not be necessary in the future.

Question 7: What formula will you use to value the business?

The formula that is used in the profession to valuate the business is, first of all, to add up the net earnings from the past three years. Divide that sum by three. This give you the average net. It is important not to base your purchase price on just the current year's net; it could be a spike year or a year in which the market takes a dive. You want to assess the full value for the business over time, but also not allow a spike year to dictate an unreasonable high value. As a seller, you want the number to be your best number but realistic. It does no good for you to overprice the business, then have the new owner not be able to meet the expected payments.

Once you have established the average net over a three-year period you need to decide whether the business is worth one, two, three, or four times the average. Much of that determination takes into account the items we have already mentioned. What physical assets will be transferred with the business? Are there a number of larger physical assets that add value? Will cars be transferred? A moving van? What condition, age, and mileage is each vehicle? Will computers be transferred? What is their age and condition? Will they hold up for several more years, or are they older, less functional items that will need to be replaced? Are the computers already networked? What software goes with the transfer of ownership? The more items that stay with the team and the more current they are, the higher the business' value.

Will the team be staying with the new entity, or will team members leave because of the transfer? What is the direction of the business? Do the three years of history show an increase, or has the team been scaling down in anticipation of change? What is the gross income versus the net? Has the percentage of profit been consistent, or is it increasing? The higher the gross versus the net, the less the value of the business. A higher gross requires a higher commitment to the business with more limited net. Some agents show a 20 to 25 percent profit margin, while others are looking at 50 to 60 percent profitability. That number impacts the formula that substantiates the selling price.

Does the public relate to the current owner, or is the owner transparent because of the way the team functions and the business is advertised. The agreement may stipulate that you maintain a license with the team and agree to have your picture, name, and information be part of its advertising for a period of time, typically five years.

Will the owner finance the purchase? If so, what amount is required for a down payment, and what interest rate will be charged? Over what period will the payments be amortized?

If the net for a business is $100,000 and a fair amount of equipment is in place, the database is functional and the lead agent is not required to be present for the business to continue at its current level, the team will stay in place and historical earnings are consistent, then the business could likely go for $200,000 to $250,000 cash or $300,000 over time for a reasonable rate of interest. To expect $400,000, the terms would need to be outstanding, the owner would need to stay involved to assist in the transition for the first year, and business growth would need to be anticipated. Also, the source of clients would need to primarily be past clients and their referrals, and the net would need to be a large percentage of the gross.

Though there is no absolute formula, there is a range based on the criteria discussed above. At no time should a seller decide that the business is so pristine that it can command the highest multiple of the formula or more. All things are negotiable.

Should the data not be available and the systems not be in order, then the business may have no value base but only be worth referral fees paid for each transaction that comes from the former owner's sources of business. This usually means that no up-front money is paid but the former owner and the current owner work out an agreement. Such an arrangement requires the former owner to communicate with the client base and grant permission to the new owner to use the former owner's name and information in advertising. In a recent educational conference, one of the panelists had procured two agents' businesses through this method. It had worked out to the advantage of both parties. The sellers did not have the information and systems in place to define a set sales price. Each did, however, have a strong placement in the community and was excited to have someone who would work with the client database and give dollar value to the resulting transactions. It was a win-win situation for each party. The current owner said that in each set of circumstances, he ended up doubling his number of transactions.

Being able to establish value as a sales price is the optimum situation for all parties involved. Each knows what to expect. A fee is paid at a set time, and everyone's obligations are complete. Even when the sales price has no set number, after a certain time frame, the purchasing owner should not be obligated to pay referral fees.

The only situation in which fees become an ongoing obligation of the new owner is when the business becomes a shared ownership, where the former owner is involved ongoing and takes part in future planning and costs. In such cases, the two parties resolve the value of the partnership and what must be paid or what obligations need to be met. The original owner continues to have a right of ownership and continuous income as arranged by the two parties. Often, this formula is used by family members when one family member has owned the business and another family member is transitioning from team member to becoming an owner. Even in these cases, income to the original owner may be cut off at some point. As one owner put it, "My son said he was not thrilled by paying me an income forever."

Question 8: What part does gross income and net income play in the valuation?

This has been lightly touched on previously in this chapter. The more gross income required to sustain the business, the greater the risk on the part of the owner should a fluctuation in the market or a loss of team members reduce closings and income. Value is assessed on annual net income. Some agents seem to feel that annual gross income is the only important aspect of the financial picture, but some are working on a very low percentage of profit. When the gross income is large enough, a small net still gives you enough money to live on. However, maintaining a high gross to survive is a stiff requirement. A business that requires a reasonable gross income to generate a livable net income has less risk and high value.

When you move from working as an individual agent to working as a team, the profit margin will fall due to paying the staff. When the staff is functioning effectively, however, there is still plenty of profit. Many times, large teams can generate 25 to 40 percent profitability. When an agent is working alone, that percentage could be as high as 65 to 70 percent, although 70 percent would be rare. You should always strive to eliminate unnecessary expenses so that net profitability is increased through wise use of the business analysis. That quarterly evaluation is, in fact, designed to assist you with just that.

Question 9: What part does knowledge of your business sources and the percent of your business derived from each source play in valuating the business?

Each business source has its own leverage of return. If the return for one source of business is three dollars for each dollar spent, while another source of business is returning on a ten-to-one basis, then you should increase the source of business with the higher return, increasing your net profitability.

The source that generates the most business for the least cost is past clients and their referrals. This source does not require advertising, at high cost, to shotgun market to the general public. It is specific advertising with a very limited cost. When a past client refers business to you, you may do something special for that person or those people, such as invite them out to dinner. State law prohibits you from sending a referral fee larger than a certain acceptable amount, unless these people are licensed agents and the fee is sent to their broker for distribution. If your total spent for the year on keeping in touch with and marketing to your past clients is $20,000 and you close 20 transactions as a result, then the cost of doing business is $1,000 per transaction. If your average income per transactions is $6,000, then your resulting ratio of return is six to one.

When a referral comes in from another real estate agent, a referral fee is sent out upon completion of the transaction. In addition, most likely some advertising was involved for that agent to find you as the receiving agent of the referral. If the average gross income per transaction is $6,000 and the referral fee is 25 percent, then the base transaction cost is $1,500 plus whatever was spent to cause that agent to refer to you. If the advertising cost is $500 per transaction, then the cost total is $3,000, and the ratio becomes three to one.

If the source is from farming, you must know just how much money was spent in the farm area and how many transactions were closed because it. Then you must divide the income from this farm area by the number of transactions and divide the costs of farming in that area by the number of transactions. The resulting numbers will give you your return ratio on dollars spent. If each closed transaction costs $1,500 and generates $6,000 on average, then your ratio of return is four to one.

Understanding the return ratio, which is derived from knowing what sources brought in the business and the cost of bringing in the business from each source, enables you to adjust your business planning. Every effort to increase the net profitability of your business enhances its ultimate value. It also puts more money in your pocket while you own the business. It seems senseless to keep on pouring out money for potential sources of business for which you have no defined dollar return ratio. Instead, by defining your business source returns, you give a future owner greater confidence in the business' systems and design. The value goes up accordingly. The value increases because of net, percent of net, and definition of dollar return ratios for the business sources. The time you take to track and understand this portion of your business leverages into an exponential return.

Question 10: How does the quality of your database and its frequency of use affect your valuation?

Your database is one of the key components of your business' value. How you track and how you keep in touch with past clients becomes a major building block for your business. A database that is not filled in and updated becomes a useless piece of material that creates more difficulty than ease.

The purchaser will want to know how often you communicate with the individuals in the database. Do you contact them by e-mail or regular mail? Do you produce a newsletter that they can access? How often do you connect with them by phone? Each personal call placed by the team member who has had most to do with that client or other person in your sphere of influence solidifies the relationship further, tying them more tightly to the team.

When mailings take place, are they sent first-class so that undeliverable letters come back? That way the team can update the information in the database. Names can be searched now through the Internet. Calls can be made to follow up with anyone who no longer seems to be at the address or phone number in the system. Someone needs to be responsible for inputting the information into the system initially. The more information you have for each individual and/or family, the better developed your communication can be. For example, birthday cards and anniversary cards can be sent out regularly. These personal touches are important in maintaining your connection with these individuals.

In Chapter 11, I described the ordeal we went through when we purchased one business. Pulling together the information was arduous but was the only way that we could re-connect with this group of people and verify the information we had input to the database. We still find holes in the database, unless we are steadily using the system and some-one is held responsible for its status.

Without constant contact, these clients will respond in the same way the National Association of REALTORS® has indicated that they do. Within two years, they will likely forget the name of the agent with whom they worked. As with all of our memories, repeated information is remembered better. To anchor it fully takes 16 or more repetitions. The closer together information is repeated, the more soundly memories are implanted. Not reminding people that you once did business with them ensures that you will ultimately lose the opportunity to do business again.

Putting systems in place can change that situation. A high number of transactions traced to repeat business with past clients or to business with referrals from past clients gives a feeling of confidence and stability to the business. A potential buyer likely will pay more for a business whose practices engender such feelings and demonstrate that this source will likely continue as the basis for success.

Question 11: How do long-term contracts and agreements affect the value of the business?

Long-term contracts, leases, and agreements are impor-tant for business success but can also deter a future buyer if the buyer feels they are not in their best interest. We are con-stantly being introduced to newer products at better rates.

Phone service can be one of those long-term commit-ments. Cell phone service contracts, if being paid by the business, is typically for a two-year period, and costs are as-sociated with breaking the commitment. While a good idea when signed, the contract may not provide the best service for the dollar now or in the future. The amount of usage may exceed the plan and, therefore, add significant costs. Phones and phone company plans change. As quickly as phones and plans change, the individual agent's needs change, too. Today, agents can receive their e-mail, contact the Internet, take pictures, get information regarding new listings, get directions to every location, and download a list of songs for their enjoyment—all on their cell phones. All of the contacts, schedules, and information necessary to go through an active, mobile day is available in these essential devices.

If the team is in a separate location from the broker's office, your business may need a phone system. If one is in place, then the questions are: How long has it been in place, and how much did it cost? Are we still paying, and how much longer must we pay? What are the benefits of this system?

Color copy machines have been changing on a regular basis. Their ability to print in full color with high quality is improving constantly, while the cost of the machines and the printing is decreasing. The speed with which they produce color prints has been increasing dramatically. If one color printer or copier is under long-term contract, then changing to a newer, more precise machine may not be feasible.

Long-term agreements for marketing in magazines and newspapers can tie the new owner to paying for a service they don't deem worthwhile. On the other hand, a long-term agreement may ensure that a great rate is locked in.

When you enter into long-term agreements, keep in mind the possible ramifications for whoever follows you. Do the agreements benefit the next individual, and why? Depending on how the business is acquired, the new owner may be obliged to continue these contracts.

Question 12: How many years of history must you show to establish a firm sense of the value of the business?

A minimum of three years of history is needed to establish the average net income and verify the value of the business. Other aspects of the business also need to be shown so that the formula can be adjusted to reflect the whole picture of the business' worth.

Three years of tax returns will be needed to verify what has been told to the government. Three years of comparative profit and loss statements are helpful. A complete list of inventory is necessary to verify what will be transferring with the change of ownership.

We reflected earlier in this chapter that showing a three-year comparison of all listings by month, contracts written by month, and closed transactions by month gives the new owner an idea of what to expect at what point in the year. Some seasons will show stronger results than others. These comparisons along with a history of sources and their respective rates of return are essential to help the buyer understand your business, and you should update and analyze them regularly. Without this knowledge, understanding how the business is functioning is a guess and a mystery, not an established fact.

Question 13: How can you make the transition seamless for the new owner?

The approach you take in planning for and implementing the transition of ownership is very important. You need to make the transition easy on your staff so that they will not fear regarding their position. You need to have as much information and process ready for the transition as possible. If the team's name does not have to be changed with the change of ownership, things will work more smoothly. Because we are dealing with an agent's business, we are not referring to the broker's name. Our team, for example, is the Arizona Power Team. We can change team ownership without changing the team's name.

Releasing long-term contracts to coincide with the transfer of the business will help the new owner make decisions without being tied to previously designed business planning.

Making sure that the previous owner is available during the transition time frame is helpful. Training is not a step-in, step-out process. Thirty days for transition is probably a short time frame. The original owner must train the new owner on the idiosyncrasies of the business. Historical files of all team members must be complete. If personality profiles exist for each team member, such as the DiSC, then having these available would be wise. The more understanding a new owner has of the operations and the personalities involved, the more productive he or she can be in maintaining and enhancing the enterprise.

You may want to make the public perceive that a merger has taken place, even if in reality, a new owner has total control. When people see a black-and-white transition, they do not tend to give the new owner the same level of loyalty, concern, and respect. With the former owner's involvement, however, the public and other professionals tend to give more credence to the viability of the enterprise. The transition can be done in such a way that most people do not even realize that a transition has occurred, enabling a seamless transition. The public and other professionals will simply see the transition as a part of the ongoing enterprise, which it is meant to be.

Question 14: What financial options for the purchaser will you make available?

Once you have decided on the base value of the business, a method of payment must be agreed upon. Cash is always best for the seller of the business, because it involves no risk. However, the buyer may not have that much cash available.

Bank loans for purchasing a real estate sales business are not readily available, unless other collateral is used to secure the loan. Most banks do not yet see the purchase of this type of business as viable, though they are willing to fund the more traditional purchase of a broker's business. Purchasing an office provides a variety of independent agents who are committed to the broker. Taking one small step away from that to fund the purchase of an individual agency or a team does not compute for bankers. The buyer may be able to get a line of credit that is unsecured to finance business operations, but that will not come close to paying for most business purchases.

Obviously, if the price is small, then cash may be an option. Another possibility is for the buyer to send you a percentage of each transaction as a referral fee for a period of time. The referral fees may start as larger percentages and decline over time. Maybe the fee is 30 to 35 percent for two or three years, then decline to 20 percent for years four and five, and 10 percent for years six and seven. The idea is that, as the years go by, the former owner has less influence on past clients' decisions to do business with the new agent.

This system is ideal for the buyer, who only pays a purchase price when a transaction actually closes. The buyer would undoubtedly be willing to pay another agent for a referral. Here, the referrals are guaranteed all to come to one source, and the marketing to those most likely to do business with the original agent is a comarketing campaign.

This leaves us with a discussion of an outright purchase by a buyer who does not have the cash or does not want to make a cash payment for the business. After determining that there will be payments over time, the price needs to be adjusted to reflect this fact. Also, the interest rate must be acceptable to the IRS. The only time that an interest rate would not be imputed by the IRS is when a family member purchases the enterprise. IRS guidelines set a minimum interest rate based on current interest expectations in the marketplace. Your accountant can give you the information regarding these numbers. This is a commercial loan and should reflect a commercial loan basis. The amortization of the loan can be long term with a balloon or can be short term as a payoff.

One of the purchases my partner and I made did not include an interest rate. We adjusted the sales price, thinking that was sufficient. Imagine our chagrin when our accountant that year asked for the interest rate and we told him there was none. He had us have the seller come see him, because there were tax consequences that neither of us had anticipated. We learned at that point that having other professionals assist us in designing any future contracts might be wise.

Our most recent purchase has a commercial rate of interest. It is not double-digit, but it is high enough that we are encouraged to be sure to pay off the loan when it is due. We have chosen a short-term amortization schedule that pays off the loan in five years. Others have amortized payments over elongated time frames with a balloon at the end. This gives the new owner some room in their monthly budget for personal income. By the time the balloon is due, the business should have moved ahead heartily, and banks will have a history with the new owner that may facilitate a line of credit to pay off the note. Alternatively, the new owner may have set aside sufficient cash by then simply to pay off the balloon note when it comes due.

You may find that a buyer is willing to attach the note to some form of real estate that they have available but want to use for other purposes. In most cases, however, you work with an unsecured loan.

The most common disagreement is over what percentage of the purchase price must be made up front. It is highly recommended that this transaction not be 100 percent financed. Most often, 20 or 25 percent down is required. The more of the business the seller can acquire from the outset, the better for them. It is not always possible to obtain high percentages up front, but you may have a buyer who has the funds and does not want to be hampered by a high monthly payment. Such a buyer will put more down up front.

In one of our purchases, the payment was attached to each transaction closed. Instead of a regular monthly payment, the buyer paid a percentage of the income coming to us as team leaders. There was a target number; when that number was reached, the business had been paid off. There was also a five-year time frame with no penalty for prepayment. The business grew as we took over the reins. The retiring selling agent retired for only six weeks. He then wanted to know if he could be an agent on the team. We were excited. This gave him the freedom to travel and do the things he wanted to do without the administrative burden of the business. Other members of the team covered for him when he was away. In the end, he made more money by being an agent with the team than he had as an owner. In addition, he gained much personal freedom. With the help of the business he generated, we were able to pay him off in three years.

Financing can take place in many ways and benefit both parties. Deciding how to finance the transaction is a matter of discussion and consensus.

Question 15: What legal documents will you need for the transition?

It is very important that everything about the transition be documented. A business relationship has no place for memories of what was supposed to have happened. Memories slip and are adjusted. Sometimes, those who were initially involved change. Estates may try to modify the buyer's original intentions. A written contract brings everything into focus and saves friendships and business relationships. It provides the clarity needed in a sometimes foggy world. Professionals who are used to putting these documents together can assist you in defining more aspects of the relationship than you thought existed.

The initial agreement is a contract with many parts. How will the entity be purchased? What part will the original owner play in the transition? How long will that individual be physically present in the business? What part will he or she play in the new organization?

The type of purchase is important, affecting the nature of the business arrangement between buyer and seller. One type is considered an asset purchase. With this method, everything, including "blue sky" (the goodwill of the business, an ethereal factor), is given a value, and this list of assets is purchased. If the current business is a corporation, the stock is not purchased. Anything done in the name of the corporation is still the corporation's responsibility.

The other type of purchase is a stock purchase in which the buyer gains all of the assets and the liabilities of the corporation. In this way, all of the contracts for services from outside vendors can stay intact. Others in the community accept the transition more easily because the entity is the same. This method is not preferred by most people representing buyers. The asset purchase is considered cleaner and precludes many legal responsibilities from falling into the sphere of the new buyer.

Technically, the asset purchase produces a new entity, so the legal liabilities of past actions still fall on the original entity. That entity stays intact for legal purposes, but its assets are transferred.

The contract itself will seem staggering at first. The documentation required as backup for the contract will cause many trees to be taken down and ground into pulp. We have two huge binders filled with documentation that both parties indicate they have looked over and have accepted. The documentation includes copies of all long-term agreements, tax returns, equipment lists, licenses, any material that will be a possible point of concern later, and a table of contents so you know which of the thousands of pages you need to find the answer to a given question. This is the material you will fall back on if a disagreement occurs. It is imperative that you keep these copies in a safe location so that they are readily available should a question arise.

The documentation is immense and will take a good deal of time to bring together. It will take some negotiation to complete. It will not be accomplished in a week or a month. The two parties must understand that these documents need to be complete and in place prior to a transition. You may set your time frame based on your expectations, but those preparing all of the documentation may have a different time frame involved. It is important to work well with the other professionals who assist you in putting this transaction together. The task will not be easy and will take effort on your part. You must be alert to what your advisors are telling you. You also need to know that this is still a new area for all of the parties involved. You must be alert to things that they might miss or mistakenly make assumptions about, because your business is not one they most likely will have been involved in selling before.

Be sure you understand, mark up, and ask questions about the first draft of any contract or document you see. This cannot simply be left to the other professionals without your input. Using professionals in other fields to guide you through this process does cost money. However, if you choose not to utilize the experience of these professionals and embark on your own, your cost can be much greater. The documents they assist in creating are the parameters by which you live during and after this transition.

Question 16: What is your time commitment once the transition is made?

One of the businesses that we purchased was interesting in that the owner discussed the possibility of selling the business and being gone in 30 days. Thirty days is not enough time, in my estimation, to negotiate the terms of the contract and have the appropriate documents drawn up and filed.

Once this owner had given some thought to the process, he determined that he would be directly involved for several months and provide contact and support for several years. This contact would be in the form of phone calls and e-mails, so the amount of time spent physically in the business full-time would be only those few initial months.

In every case where we have purchased a business, the amount of time required on the part of the seller of the business has been those first three to six months. In one case, I assisted with the sale of a business in which the owner agreed to one year of direct involvement. The first six months were full-time, and the second six months were three days a week.

In many cases, the owners are requested to come back to the area for special events, such as client parties and other public activities. The more the transition is supposed to look like a merger, the more time and effort is required from the original owner. The amount of time the former owner spends with the business dramatically affects the transition and the public's response.

Should the transition actually be a merger or new partnership, the amount of time the original owner needs to spend involved in the business still must be agreed upon. In these situations, whether it is family transition or a nonrelative transition, the new partner needs to understand why he needs to take on this responsibility. Most often, the original owner's personal agenda is to spend more time in another pursuit. Travel, hobbies, and a desire to provide service to the community are three of the most dominant themes. Sometimes, a second business opportunity requires the previous owner's time. The amount of time required of each party needs to be stipulated and written out. That way, no misunderstandings can arise about the nature of the agreement.

Defining the amount of time the seller will spend in the business is important. Defining the amount of time that must be spent outside the business in the marketplace is also important. This information is detailed in a noncompete clause. The original owner guarantees not to work as a licensed member of any other organization involved in real estate sales in the same geographic territory as the current business. In addition, all leads that the original owner has for real estate sales are to be given to the new owner, typically with no referral fee, because the new owner is already paying for that business. This clause is especially important if the original owner has relatives in the business in that area.

In addition, a written agreement about any names, titles, Web sites, pictures, and any other form of identification staying with the original team is important. The last thing a buyer wants to see is the associated family name being advertised by a son, daughter, or other family member, directing the public's attention away from the business.

Question 17: How do you find a successor?

One way to find a successor to your business is to give birth to that individual. Many family businesses are passed from generation to generation. The obvious concern is over family infighting if multiple offspring are involved. If three children all want to go into the business, how do you decide which one to put in charge or which ones will work together as a management team?

If only one child is involved, you must determine that the others do not have an interest in taking over the business. Agreements must be made in writing as to what that means to the members of the family and to the estate of the original owner. It may seem strange to talk about the estate, but family feuds have started over much smaller sources of wealth. Some will consider the business a family asset, while others will understand the amount of time one or more family members have spent in the development of the business. Please preempt family issues by defining what is to happen.

The second method of identifying a successor is to hire that person and train him. This method generally creates an easy transition for the new owner because of the already existing relationship between the owners in the public eye. The most common difficulties that seem to arise in these situations concern the value of the business and the amount the new owner must pay to own or become a co-owner of the business. If the new owner is aware early on that this relationship may develop into a partnership and ultimately ownership, then he may feel that his time spent in the business is investment enough and may not feel a need to pay money for the opportunity. If the terms of the transition are defined in advance, making sure that the desires of the original owner are fulfilled and the new owner agrees, then friction is less likely.

Often, the original owner is looking for some affiliation, though minor in terms of time spent. The original owner is also normally looking for a perpetual income to fund their retirement or semiretirement. How long will this income be paid? At what point will the price be fulfilled? If the original owner dies, what responsibility does the new owner have to the estate? If a buyout will occur after a period of partnership, how will the price and terms be determined?

Be certain that you know whom you have hired and his or her strengths. I had in mind that I would give an opportunity to a staff member who had supported me well for nine years. I thought she would be the one to take over the business. I made the terms very easy for her. I gave her plenty of time to get the feel of the business before fees would begin flowing to me. I simply forgot the fact that she was a high S: she was very supportive and excelled in support positions, but she really did not want to take center stage. For the first year and a half, she excelled, making a great deal of money and being named rookie of the year for the company's Illinois region. But I could tell over the phone that she was feeling excessive pressure. She finally called and said she needed to be released from our contract. Because of our friendship, I did just that. Promoting her had been my idea, and I had chosen improperly. My goals were worthy, and she did not want to disappoint. That was a part of her nature as an S personality. She was not, however, comfortable in the role.

Be sure that a leadership role is in the best interest of the person to whom you entrust your business. After a year to two years in someone else's hands, my business no longer had value to others in the real estate community. I have ended up simply referring leads and obtaining referral fees for that venture. She ended up as a trusted team member of another top agent who had been a part of our team for a short time.

The third way is to find someone who is in the field of real estate who wants to add your business to his existing business or wants to move to the area and jump-start his entry. This can be the scariest form of selling your business. You may not know this person very well. Unless you have worked alongside the individual, you may not know his business practices and his level of integrity. In such a case, you should get to know others who have known this individual for quite some time. You also need to spend some time talking with the individual and getting a sense of his intentions. The two of you need to come to some agreements in pursuing the concept of a sale.

Finding this individual may be less difficult than you think. If you are involved with other agents whom you trust on a national level, then you may want to let them know that you are beginning a search. The laws of attraction seem to work well here. If you prepare to sell your business, very likely someone in the vicinity wants to begin or expand a business in your area. Placing an ad in the newspaper or on Monster.com is probably not a good idea. Instead, making discreet inquiries among professionals in the area, and among the vendors you use, may give you the lead you are looking for. Attorneys, lenders, and title company employees may have suggestions for you. Be sure to reinforce their concern for your privacy by not broadcasting your request for their help.

Question 18: How do you qualify the successor?

If the successor is a relative, you should have a good idea of their ability to follow through on commitments. It is important that you work on what you know about their capacities instead of what you feel about them because they are related. Remember that I made a mistake in judgment that cost me the value of the business in Chicago. I never want to make that mistake again. Please be cautious about the opportunity you are presenting to this family member.

When the person is an employee, you should have a feel for their trustworthiness. I have found that some employees feel entitled to your business because they have worked for you. They may even feel that, somehow, they have been the creator of your business. More than a few individuals over the years, after working for me for a time, were sure that they could exceed my results on their own. Only a few still survive in the industry. Many have gone by the wayside. Some were finished with the business in only a few months.

You should fully understand the intentions and qualifications of a person coming in from outside of your sphere of experience and family affiliation. You need to know their financial history. If you will not be fully paid up front, then you need to go through the same process a bank would go through. You need to feel comfortable that they have a history of paying bills and not overextending themselves. You also need to feel that they will enhance and not degrade your business. After all, you want that business to pay you the dividends you have earned.

Just as you provide financial information for their consideration, they should provide information in return. At least request a personal net worth statement and three years of tax returns. You are also well within your rights to request support letters from those with whom they have had business dealings. They should not find such a request surprising or insulting.

Question 19: What transition problems do you see with your team? With the public?

Transition problems with the team result from their discomfort with the new team leader. If the new owner is a relative or someone currently on the team, then you can easily see their daily interaction with the team. If you see that the transition will be difficult, then you may need to assist others in making decisions for their future prior to the transition. You want as many seasoned team members in place as possible when the transition occurs, so that the transition is as seamless as possible with no emergency hiring and training.

One problem that can be anticipated is if a member of the team wants to be the new team leader. If someone is of the opinion that they are the one in line to take that position and feel overlooked, then they may set out to undermine the team and its performance. Knowing your team members well enough to anticipate this possibility will alleviate a great deal of team dysfunction. Replacing such a person early on could help a lot. Otherwise, the team may split between those who favor that individual and those who favor the one you selected.

Other difficulties can arise if the new team leader makes immediate, radical changes to the way the team functions. Certain modifications will occur simply because of personality differences. However, major changes that occur prior to the staff's becoming comfortable with the new leader can cause turmoil.

The public will notice if, all of a sudden, the advertising adopts a completely different flair. The public presentation of the transition needs to be planned to entice them to continue to do business with the same entity they are accustomed to doing business with. The name, the faces involved, and the perception of the entity in the community need to be consistent with what they have seen. Initial changes should be subtle and new players introduced gradually. Competing real estate professionals will try to capitalize on any change they perceive.

Question 20: What are the ramifications of selling the business under each scenario?

Defining what would happen under each of the preceding scenarios is important. If the business is sold to a family member, will it still be an asset purchase? Or will it be a stock purchase with all things remaining intact? If a person who has been on the team is involved, how will the rest of the team perceive their promotion? Have they known for a while that this where you've been headed? If another outside party is involved, will this person take over under a stock purchase plan or execute an asset purchase, engendering some name changes and modifications?

You should discuss the tax ramifications of the sale of stock versus assets with your accountant. Having an unsecured note as the basis for the majority of a buyer's payout to you may be a concern for your attorney. Having a family member conduct a stock purchase may leave you liable for things they do in the name of the business.

The ramifications of each scenario are so different that you need to sit down with your professional consultants from other fields to ponder the ultimate results. From tax consequences to legal responsibilities, making different decisions causes different outcomes. The interest rate required by the IRS was one thing I missed on one of my contracts. Fortunately, with the advice of our accountant, we reached an understanding with the seller that was acceptable to all.

Not everything is as clearly defined. Our attorney did not understand the ramifications of having tail insurance for errors and omissions (E&O) coverage when we changed brokers. It had been discussed amongst the participants, but when it was not fully laid out in the contract, questions arose as to the decision that had been agreed to verbally. Because of the integrity of the individuals involved, the misunderstanding was not a major disaster. It could have been a major demoralizing force between the seller and ourselves; it only became a nonissue due to the relationship that had been developed and the honesty with which each party entered the agreement.

Question 21: What is your legal responsibility after the sale?

Your legal responsibilities depend on the type of sale. You will incur many further obligations under an asset sale for commitments made by the previous entity. Because you are selling assets and not liabilities, you must finish any obligations under those terms.

If you are purchasing another business as a part of your business plan, then you have a variety of obligations as the new owner, which are spelled out in your agreement. Not the least of these will be the payment of the purchase price to the seller in the time frame outlined in the contract and financial agreement.

As the original owner, you should keep tabs on the business for at least as long as the purchase price remains unpaid. Should the price not be paid, then reacquiring the team is your recourse. What that entails is found in those many documents I have told you to pay careful attention to. The question is: After what period of time will an entity of some value still exist for you can take back? I was out of the area for about a year while my business was run by someone else. Staff was let go. Advertising campaigns were neglected. Reenergizing the business when I had another business going in another state was too difficult. I chose to move on and learn from my mistake. If I had originally chosen to structure the deal by making my buyer a partner to someone who wanted to take charge out front, the transition might have been very successful. She definitely had the capability to support whoever was out front. The part of the business that she disliked, that of being out front, would have been handled by another person.

Question 22: What specialists can guide you through the process?

You definitely need an attorney whose specialty is business acquisitions. Someone who already deals in this area has the experience to tell you what is normally done. Your acquisition is likely smaller than the average transaction the attorney handles. You need to know the price for the attorney's services. This individual should create the document, with the other party's attorney being the respondent, to allow your side to direct the structure of the deal. Still, the other attorney will suggest changes to benefit their client. Be sure to understand the impact of any suggested change.

Because you will live with this document for the duration of the relationship, you need to understand every section. Even if the answer is, "This is just standard language," you need to understand what that standard language means and what obligations it imposes on you. You'll need to involve your accountant and other advisors, so find out what the cost will be for their services. One suggestion is that you attend all these meetings so you can see where each advisor is coming from. You will have a clearer understanding of the whole when you understand all of the parts.

The second advisor I recommend is an accountant. Again, having an accountant with experience in the field of business acquisition is advantageous. Certainly they will be able to analyze the business and make suggestions for the agreement. The new owner will undoubtedly have an accountant meet on a monthly or at least quarterly basis to review the current status of the business and make recommendations to enhance profitability or change decisions in light of their tax implications.

The third professional that I suggest you hire is someone who will help you to see the opportunity of valuing and selling your real estate business. This person is a very specialized individual, and not many people have a lot of experience in the business. When you are introduced to someone who has credentials for assisting you in this area, you should find out how many times this person has successfully assisted others. The analysis of the business is more complex than the simple formula makes it look. The nuances of the business and the implications of historical data must be understood. Displays of historical information must be developed to influence another to take the plunge and purchase your business.

The valuation of a business may be for a fixed amount of money and may take a specific amount of time. If you have detailed data available, that time frame can be met comfortably. If you are not keeping current records, however, then additional time will be needed to accrue and interpret the information. Your staff may be able to fulfill the requested information flow after initial contact.

If someone needs to come into your community and spend a day to several days preparing the information, there will be an additional cost. If valuation of the business were to cost $5,000, for example, and two days were required to come into town and help prepare the material, you would incur a two-day charge plus transportation and accommodations. Many people cringe at the thought of paying these fees. If the individual will actually be assisting with the sale, then they will also charge a fee for that service, typically a percent of the sale value. This often includes coaching the new owner for a year to help them become established with your business.

When I was first selling my business, a business broker specializing in agent business sales approached me. We had been friends for some time. He said he would assist me in the process. I could not see that much was involved. He said the cost would be a percentage of the sale price. I staggered at what he had just told me and responded that I could probably handle it myself. His comment has stuck with me all of these years: "If you choose not to pay me for my services, you will, in the end, pay for not having used my services." The reproach stung initially. However, by not having using the guidance of an experienced person, I have paid many times more than his counsel would have cost me.

By not using these professionals in the valuation, documentation, and financial interpretation of the business, you will lose way more than credible professional counsel costs. Having your own attorney, accountant, and business sales advisor creates an environment in which you can feel confident of achieving your goal.

Question 23: How do you maintain a separation between the value of the business and the value of any real estate being purchased simultaneously with the business?

Though unlikely, a purchase of a building may occur simultaneously with the purchase of the business. These two items need to be handled as totally separate matters. The value of the building may fluctuate if the value is based on owner occupancy and the new owner of the business is not prepared to stay at that location.

The seller then has the opportunity to decide if it is necessary to tie both together. Their decision will depend partly on the value of property and rents in the area. We are assuming here that the real estate being purchased is the office location of the business. If not, then there is no need to relate the two. If so, then an agreement needs to be clarified between buyer and seller as to the necessity of the real estate purchase being simultaneous with the business purchase.

It may be that a lease can keep the entity in that location until such time as a purchase of the real estate can be consummated. The terms of that agreement may be set up currently or reflect the need to have an appraisal at the time of the purchase. Documents may reference each other, but the contract, if any, for the real estate needs to be separate from the contract for the business.

Summary

If you are just beginning to embark in the field of real estate sales, you will be able to establish your business with the end in mind. By systematizing your business initially, you will be able to run more smoothly and more profitably for its duration. Preparing to exit the business is not a process to be left for the end of your professional career. By doing regular assessments, quarterly reviews and adjustments, and annual summations, you will know what your business is doing and take the next appropriate step each year.

Annual business planning is the means of understanding who you are as a businessperson and how your asset is doing. You cannot become as proficient as you need to be by winging your career. Careful business analysis and specific business planning will be the key to maximizing your profit margins and building an asset with great intrinsic worth.

By careful record keeping and tracking, you will be able to shift the sails of this ship of which you are the captain. You will be able to direct its speed. You will be able to keep her off the rocky shoals that could sink her. Knowing the direction of the winds of financial change in your area and in the country, you will be able to keep her headed in the right direction. When storms arise, you will know where to draw into port. Therefore, you will be one of the first back on the water when times are right again.

When you find that the time is at hand to serve as captain no longer, you will be able to turn the helm over to someone who is capable of steering the vessel. You will provide for another the freedom that you have so comfortably enjoyed all these years. In the meantime, you will find new adventures and opportunities—available because of how well you kept the ship.

At the end of your real estate career, you will look back at the places your ship has carried you. You will marvel at the views, the sunsets, and the sunrises you have enjoyed. You will remember the waves that have brought you peace and the ones that caused you to draw upon your greatest skills. All of these memories depend on the choices you make now. Most of those who enter this career will not reap the rewards that can be yours. The course you chart now will determine your destination.

The choice is yours. Choose well.

Appendix

Notes/Ideas

_____
_____
_____
_____
_____
_____
_____
_____
_____
_____
_____
_____
_____
_____
_____
_____
_____

Notes/Ideas

Notes/Ideas

Agent Closed Transaction Count

TARMLS 2005: 6536 MLS Members

Where exactly do you fall as a member of the Tucson Multiple Listing Service?

NUMBER of AGENTS in TARMLS	NUMBER of TRANSACTIONS CLOSED
2644	0
526	1
494	2
391	3
299	4
245	5
196	6
168	7
189	8
129	9
126	10
111	11
112	12
98	13
75	14
73	15
69	16
50	17
45	18
40	19
38	20
34	21
33	22
25	23
18	25
284	**OVER 25**

Gross Income Projections

Net Personal Expenses   _____

Gross Business Expenses   _____

Gross Income Requirement (GIR)   _____

Anticipated Average Sales Price   _____

Anticipated Average Commission %   _____

Anticipated Gross Commission $ _____

Anticipated Net Commission $
After Splits (ANC$)   _____

Number of Anticipated Transactions
(GIR/ANC$)   _____

Number of Listings Sold   _____

    Number of Listings Taken   _____

Number of Buyers Sold   _____

    Number of Buyers Worked With   _____

Personal Expenses: The "Have To's" . . .

Category of Payment	Payment	# of Payments per Year	Total Annual Expense
Cable/Satellite			
Car Payment			
Car Maintenance			
Child Care			
Clothing			
Computer Connection			
Donations			
Education			
Entertainment			
Food			
Gas-Auto			
Gifts			
Home Owners Association			
Home Maintenance			
House Payment/Rent			
Insurance Auto			
Insurance Dental			
Insurance Home			
Insurance Life			
Insurance Medical			
Investment/Savings			
Retirement			
Taxes Income			
Taxes Real Estate			
Utilities Electric			
Utilities Gas			
Utilities Water			
Utilities Phone			
Vacations			
Other			
Gross Personal Expenses			
Other Income Source			
Net Personal Expense			

Business Budget Analysis From _____, 200__ To _____, 200__

Item	Budget	Year to Date	% Difference
Advertising Expense			
Adv Business Cards			
Adv Business Fliers			
Adv Car Magnets			
Adv Int GoToMyPC			
Adv Int Best Image			
Adv Int Network Solutions			
Adv Int WhereToLive			
Adv Kitchen Implements			
Adv Magnetic Calendar			
Adv Newsletter Continental Ranch			
Adv Newspaper Homes and Land			
Adv Billboards—Homes and Land			
Adv Newspaper Harmon Homes			
Adv Newspaper Marana Chamber			
Adv Newspaper Monument News			
Adv Newspaper Tucson Newspaper			
Adv Newspaper Custom House			
Adv Notepads			
Adv Printing Color Printer			
Adv Printing Marathon			
Adv Shirts			
Adv Signs			
Adv Wrap Vehicles			
Auto Truck			
Auto Honda			
Auto Gas			
Auto Toyota 05			
Bank and Credit Card Charges			
Charitable Contributions			
Contract Labor			
Customer Satisfaction			
Dues and Subscriptions			
Equipment Expense			
Gifts			
Gifts Closing Candle			
Gifts Staff			
Home Warranty			
Insurance Expense			

Continued on next page . . .

Business Budget Analysis From _____, 200___ To _____, 200___

Insurance Health Expense			
Interest Expense			
Internet—Other			
Legal and Professional Expense			
Licenses Expense			
Maintenance Expense			
Meals and Entertainment Exp			
Postage Expense			
Professional Development			
Professional Services			
Promotion			
Promotional Customer Appreciation			
Property Management Expense			
Rent or Lease Expense			
Shared Office and Desk Fee			
Software Expense			
Supplies			
Telephone Expense			
Travel Expense			
Travel Air Fare			
Travel Lodging			
Travel Meals			
Travel Rental Cars			
Travel Gas			
Travel Taxis, Trains, Limos, etc.			
RE/MAX Copies			
RE/MAX Management Fees and Dues			
RE/MAX Advertising Expense			
RE/MAX Gifts			
Wages Payroll Tax Expense			
Wages Expense			
Total Expenses			
Number of transactions			
Average price of transaction			
Average percent of commission			
Average income per transaction			
Gross Team Income			
Team Members Income			
Rainmaker's Income			
Rainmaker's Net Income			

EXIT Strategy Questionnaire

1. How will you know when it is time to leave the real estate business?

2. What part does an annual business plan play in the preparation of your business for transition?

3. At what point do you start preparing for your exit?

4. What systems need to be in place in order to have a smooth transition? (The McDonald's Theory)

5. What are the assets you will have available for a successor?

6. What will you need to have in place to show the value of the business?

7. What formula will you use to value the business?

8. What part does Gross Income and Net Income play in valuation?

9. What part does a knowledge of your business sources and the percent of your business derived from each play in valuating the business?

10. How does the current level of your database and its frequency of use in contacting past clients and sphere of influence affect your valuation?

11. How do long-term contracts and agreements affect the value of the business? (i.e., leases, advertising agreements, financing of equipment purchases)

12. How many years of history will you need to show in order to give a firm feeling for the value of the business?

13. How can you make the transition seamless for the new owner?

14. What financial options for the purchaser are you willing to make available?

15. What legal documents will you need for the transition?

16. What is your time commitment once the transition is made?

17. How do you find the successor?

18. How do you qualify as a successor?

19. What transition problems do you see with your team? With the public?

20. What are the tax ramifications for selling the business under each scenario?

21. What is your legal responsibility after the sale?

22. Who are the specialists who can guide you through the process?

23. How do you maintain a separation between the value of the business and the value of any real estate being purchase simultaneously with the business?

Daily Sources of Leads Log

Date	Internet	Signs	Post Cards	Homes and Land	Monument News	COI	Past Client	Past Client Ref	Family	Agent Referral	Vendor Referral	Farming	Cold Calling

Transactions Pending

MLS #	Address	List Price	Sale Price	Contract Date	Close Date	L/S	Sale	Net Comm	Source

Transactions Closed Report

Year 2005

MONTH	LISTINGS SOLD	SALES	TOTAL
January			
February			
March			
April			
May			
June			
July			
August			
September			
October			
November			
December			
TOTAL			

Year 2006

MONTH	LISTINGS SOLD	SALES	TOTAL
January			
February			
March			
April			
May			
June			
July			
August			
September			
October			
November			
December			
TOTAL			

Year 2007

MONTH	LISTINGS SOLD	SALES	TOTAL
January			
February			
March			
April			
May			
June			
July			
August			
September			
October			
November			
December			
TOTAL			

Listings Taken Yearly Report

LISTINGS TAKEN

YEAR	2005	2006	2007	2008
January				
February				
March				
April				
May				
June				
July				
August				
September				
October				
November				
December				
TOTAL				

Gross Income Yearly Report

GROSS INCOME

Month	2006	2007	2008	2009	2010
January					
February					
March					
April					
May					
June					
July					
August					
September					
October					
November					
December					
TOTAL					
EXPENSE					
NET PROFIT					

3 Year Average _____

Net Value _____

Written Transactions Report

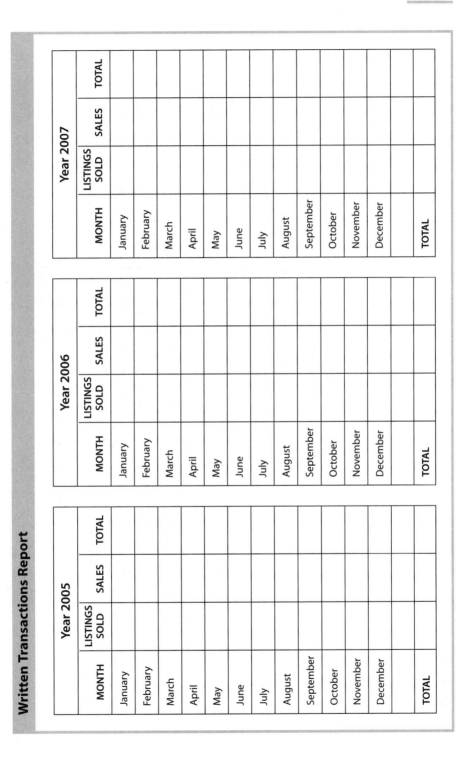

Year 2005

MONTH	LISTINGS SOLD	SALES	TOTAL
January			
February			
March			
April			
May			
June			
July			
August			
September			
October			
November			
December			
TOTAL			

Year 2006

MONTH	LISTINGS SOLD	SALES	TOTAL
January			
February			
March			
April			
May			
June			
July			
August			
September			
October			
November			
December			
TOTAL			

Year 2007

MONTH	LISTINGS SOLD	SALES	TOTAL
January			
February			
March			
April			
May			
June			
July			
August			
September			
October			
November			
December			
TOTAL			

Inventory Listing Log

MLS #	Address	List Date	Exp Date	Source	List Price	SF	T/C	MSF	Land	Sold	Expired	Released

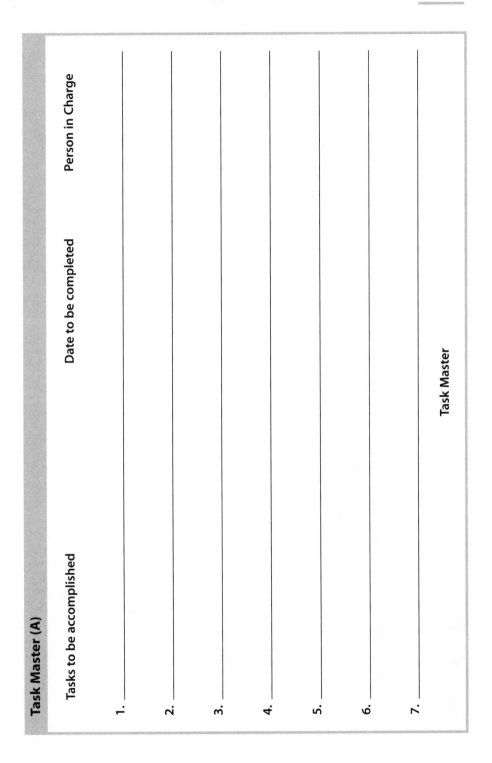

Task Master (A)

Tasks to be accomplished	Date to be completed	Person in Charge
1.		
2.		
3.		
4.		
5.		
6.		
7.		

Task Master

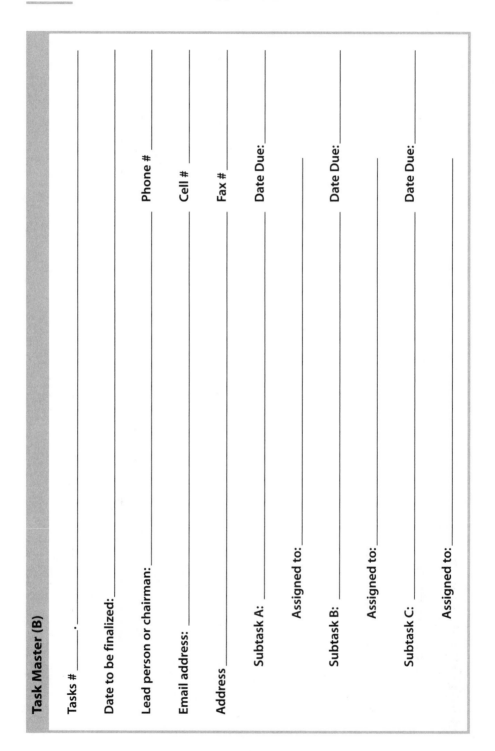

Task Master (B)

Tasks # _____ . _____

Date to be finalized: _____

Lead person or chairman: _____   Phone # _____

Email address: _____   Cell # _____

Address _____   Fax # _____

Subtask A: _____   Date Due: _____

   Assigned to: _____

Subtask B: _____   Date Due: _____

   Assigned to: _____

Subtask C: _____   Date Due: _____

   Assigned to: _____

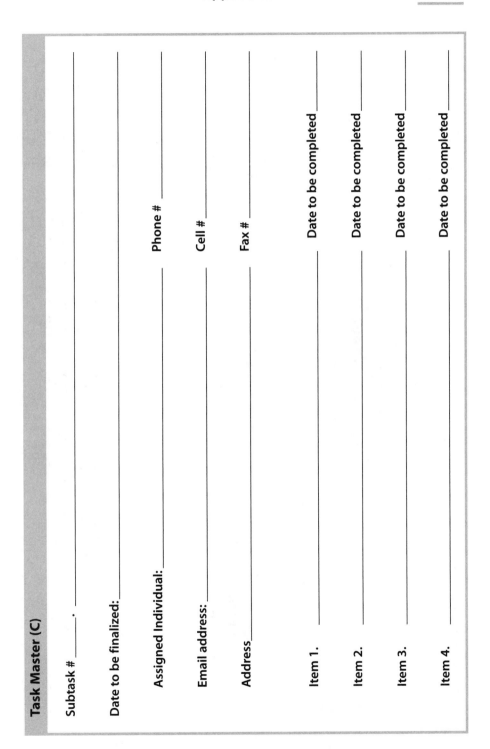

Task Master (C)

Subtask # _____ . _____

Date to be finalized: _____

Assigned Individual: _____   Phone # _____

Email address: _____   Cell # _____

Address _____   Fax # _____

Item 1. _____   Date to be completed _____

Item 2. _____   Date to be completed _____

Item 3. _____   Date to be completed _____

Item 4. _____   Date to be completed _____

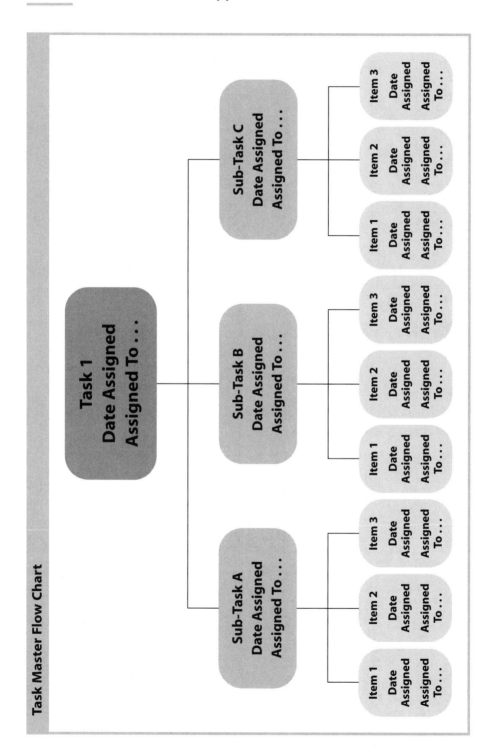

Index

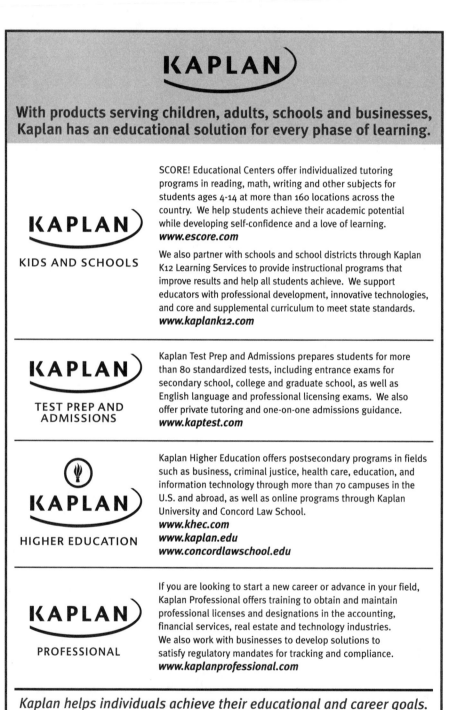